HOUSE OF
NEW BEGINNINGS

Also by Frank Wilson

COUNSELLING THE DRUG ABUSER

HOUSE OF
NEW BEGINNINGS

by
Frank W. Wilson

with Linda Ball

LAKELAND, Marshall, Morgan & Scott, a member of the Pentos group, 1 Bath Street, London EC1V 9LB. Copyright © Frank Wilson 1977. First published 1977. ISBN 0 551 00776 1. All rights reserved. Printed in Great Britain by Hunt Barnard Printing Ltd., Aylesbury, Bucks.

To Shirley

Introduction

The church service had been all that a visiting preacher could hope for. From the crowded congregation people had streamed forward to kneel at the altar rail in response to my appeal to them to become Christians or to re-dedicate their lives to God.

'Brother,' said one of the church elders, 'this *must* be the place God wants you to be.'

I nodded, my heart bursting with joy. Bradford, and a big, welcoming church for my very own pastorate. It would mean an end to the hand-to-mouth existence Shirley and I had known for so long. It would mean security and fulfilment.

An hour later I had just finished counselling the last of the many enquirers when a long-haired young man came in. His thin body seemed to shrink into his old leather jacket; his face was pale and his eyes stared into the distance. He looked frightened, yet vague.

'Did you want to talk to me?' I asked.

He focused on me slowly, his gaze like that of a lost animal, hurt and lonely.

'You said this Jesus could set the drug addict free,' he blurted out. 'Well, I'm one. What about me?'

In that moment I knew this was my sign from God. Not the big church, for all its opportunities. My work was to be back in London, with the drug addicts I'd been waiting there to find. London, where this boy had first got caught up with the evil crowd of drug pushers who had reduced him to this state. He had run away to Bradford to escape, he told me, but it was too late. He was hooked.

As I talked to young Michael that night he took off his jacket and showed me the scars of addiction that I would see often in the future – blue pock marks, livid abscesses and the vein tracks that identified him as a mainliner – one who took his drugs intravenously. Jagged white lines around his wrists told of his attempt to take his own life.

I reached out and put my hands on his scarred arms.

'Lord Jesus, you shed your blood to set men free from sin. I pray that you will heal the wounds on Michael's body, mind and spirit which have been caused by drugs.'

There were tears on Michael's face now, but a new light was coming into his eyes.

'I feel different! Free!'

There were tears in my eyes, too, as I hugged him and gave thanks to God. Lord, send me to the Michaels of this world, I silently prayed. Send me to the Michaels.

I

I don't suppose I had any idea of what I was letting myself in for, that day back in my mid-teens when I decided to become a Christian. For me it was not just a question of turning over a new leaf and going to church. It was the start of a whole new life. With all the enthusiasm of a seventeen-year-old I threw myself into Christian work, taking preaching appointments and studying hard to enter the ministry.

I was a young Baptist pastor when I met and married Shirley, my helpmate who has been at my side through all these succeeding years. Life was not easy in those early days; the church could only afford a part-time salary and even with both of us doing various other jobs we were often short of money. But we gave the church work first priority; I took on jobs like delivering meat at 4 a.m. and somehow we struggled through. When our first baby arrived we were thrilled, but of course Shirley's earnings stopped, and now and then, because we were so young, we made bad mistakes – like the time we ran up a huge bill.

We had no experience of living in an all-electric house, so neither of us thought of economising. When our first bill came in it was for the then massive sum of thirty pounds! Aghast, we prayed for forgiveness for our extravagance and asked God to meet the bill.

The following Sunday saw a man in our church whose nephew I had been able to help. Quietly he slipped an envelope into Shirley's hand. It contained thirty-three pounds – all we needed and some over, which we joyfully gave to the Lord's work. We were learning to live by faith in God, like trusting children grasping a father's hand.

One day a well-known evangelist named Edgar Trout came to our area. Healed by God of a crippling illness, Edgar had become a man to whom God clearly spoke in a very personal way. In fact he was used by God to bring a special message to me.

God was going to lead me into a new and marvellous ministry, I learned. It would be a ministry of healing broken lives, reaching all the world. There would be misunderstandings, sorrows and disappointments, but God would give me a wisdom beyond my years . . . I listened as Edgar Trout told me these things; humbled and awed, I could only believe and trust God for further guidance.

Soon I felt I must leave the church ministry and become an evangelist. I became involved with young people, college students as well as the roughs and toughs of the district, and there was great joy in knowing they were being helped. Life was still far from easy for Shirley and me, though; we lived in temporary homes offered by friends and were as hard-up as ever. Yet when the chance of a well-paid job with an animal-feed firm came along I knew I must turn it down. I dared not tie myself to a large business company and put God's work in second place.

The evening when I made that decision is clear in memory. Shirley and I put little Christina to bed and then we sat on the top stair and prayed, our arms around each other. We knew we might soon be homeless again, with no money and with another baby on the way. Yet our hearts were full of confidence. We would go on putting God first in our lives. He would provide; we knew it.

One day the post brought an invitation to me to attend a ministers' meeting in London on the subject of witchcraft and devil worship in Britain, and I saw with interest that the speaker was to be Edgar Trout. The invitation reminded me of his prophecy about me, and as I travelled up to London to the meeting I stared unseeingly from the window, wondering about the future. What could this ministry among young people of which he had spoken really be? Surely it was not just the work I was doing among the students? No, Edgar had said it would be a specific ministry to young people with broken, empty lives. Well, I knew there were plenty of grave social problems among the young generation.

I held out my ticket mechanically and the inspector clipped it briskly and passed on. I was remembering an article I'd read recently about a little-known Christian minister working on the streets of New York among young people who were addicted to drugs. My heart went cold as I thought about it, my mind conjuring up pictures of unshaven criminal types and gangsters brandishing knives and chains in the filthy streets of a New York ghetto area. Was it really like that, or had I just been watching too many television films? I remembered the minister's name. David Wilkerson. He must be a man of great courage, I thought. But that was America. Britain was different. We had no great drug problem like that.

The train pulled into Charing Cross station with a jolt and I realised that all the other passengers had buttoned up their coats and were already out of their seats and pushing along the corridor. I bowed my head and closed my eyes for a few seconds. 'Dear Lord,' I whispered, 'I want to be useful to you, really useful.' I stood up and pulled my briefcase off the luggage rack and made my way off the train.

I found myself battling against streams of people on their way out of London after their day's work. The station was a sea of people surging forward on to the platforms.

'The train about to leave Platform Seven is the 6.38 to . . . Come here . . . Come here, Frank, to this place . . . Come . . . '

I stopped dead in my tracks, the crowd jostling from behind and pushing roughly past my shoulders. I stared at the faces around me – some serious and intent, some determined, some tense and angry. But obviously not one of them was hearing what I was. It was almost as if the announcing system had suddenly been taken over. But no, it was the voice of God coming to me, soft, low and sweet and drowning all else. 'Come here, to this place. Leave all behind and come here and serve me. I want you to show young people my love and lift them out of despair.'

For a few seconds there was silence, and then back came the roar all around me, the metallic engine clanking, the rumble of the porters' trolleys, the stampede of an army's feet and, yes, the droning voice of the station announcer calling for all those who wanted the 6.38 leaving from Platform Seven . . .

I began striding towards the exit. Was it just me being emotional? Or was it really the voice of God? I felt torn

12

about, yet deep inside I was already coming to terms with the truth that God had once again intervened in my life and answered my prayers for direction. So we were to come to this place? To London?

I was just the same – or was I? Suddenly the world around was different. As I sat in the underground train I found myself staring intensely at the people around me, turning away quickly and uncomfortably when I realised that they were becoming annoyed or embarrassed under my persistent gaze. People somehow weren't just faces any more. I seemed to have a special sight, or insight, which took me beyond or inside them. I could see their spirits. I could identify the lonely, the unloved, the unhappy, the disillusioned. And some of them seemed to be dying inside. All these sad people, people empty of purpose, devoid of peace and love. But where was God? Not far away, I knew. And I knew too that God wanted to share the lives of all these, to weep with the broken-hearted, to hold the hand of the lonely. He wanted more than anything to be involved intimately with people's lives. Why had they all shut the doors on him, shut out the light? Why had men shut God out of their personal problems, out of the nation's distress, out of the political scene, out of all the complex social, psychological and medical questions of the age? Why did man in all his hollow wisdom reject God as inadequate to meet his needs?

The young woman opposite me sat on the edge of her seat, mentally driving the tube train past every station and looking angrily at her watch every few seconds, her mouth bitter and her forehead tense. Next to her a middle-aged woman in a red silk scarf studied her long painted nails and pouted with discontent. The man next to me hid his thoughts in a blank expression. These were God's creation, these people and all the millions more who locked their sorrows up inside and ached with the pain. It was only natural that God should be interested in them, should want to be involved. God wasn't just an optional extra to life for the man who wanted to feel good on Sundays. God was that something that was missing from the hearts and lives of men and women.

A thousand thoughts and images came flooding into my mind, as suddenly I seemed to become acutely aware of the desperate need that people had for God. Everywhere I looked an empty longing heart seemed to stare back, and in my ears echoed over and over again the words I'd heard on the station. 'Come to this place. Come to this place.'

The hall was crowded when I arrived, a little out of breath, and someone was making some introductory announcements. I slipped into the back row where I spotted an empty seat in a not too good position almost directly behind a pillar. After a few minutes Edgar Trout took over the microphone and began his address. I leaned forward in my seat, craning my neck to see him and catch his words.

'Before I come to my main subject of witchcraft tonight I would like to just tell you briefly what I was doing last night.'

I smiled to myself as I recognised the warm and authoritative tones of this man of God, whom I'd come to respect so much. He began to describe how he had spent the night walking around the streets of the West End of London, how he had met Christian workers and others who had shown him a whole world of despair. They had introduced him to the world of the tramps and prostitutes. In the early hours of the morning he had caught glimpses of the deepest shame and degradation. But the saddest thing of all, he said, was that there was only a handful of people taking to them the hope of the

Christian Gospel, the words of new life. Here, he went on, were people selling their bodies and souls, surrounded by physical and spiritual darkness. Drunks, homeless beggars, old and young, teenagers addicted to drugs . . .

My whole attention was caught and my heart seemed to leap inside me. So there really were young drug takers in this country after all? And was no one searching them out in the name of Jesus Christ?

'And, friends, I've got something to say tonight that's vitally important!'

The entire hall was hushed. Edgar's voice was intense, urgent.

'I believe God is speaking to a young man tonight in this very hall. He wants this young man to go and work among the lost young people on the streets of this city. A young man here tonight. God is speaking to him right now, and I want to tell him that whatever happens he must be obedient to this call.'

Nothing could have robbed me then of the certainty in my heart that the young man he was talking about was me! All the voice of Heaven itself seemed to be pleading in my ears, and my heart witnessed agreement. Yes, God was talking to me, confirming the call he'd given me just a short time ago as I'd stood amazed in the jostling crowds on Charing Cross station.

The rest of the meeting was a blur. The challenge of all that had happened was occupying the whole of me, thrilling me and yet filling me with a thousand little fears. I stood numbly for the closing prayer and then rushed to the front of the hall. I tapped Edgar on the shoulder and poured out my story, the words tumbling out in confusion.

'Brother,' he said, nodding his head as I came to the end of my story, 'Brother, if God has really spoken to you,

you see that you do what he says.'

That night Shirley and I knelt and asked God to give us a home for his work – a home in London.

The chance soon afterwards to talk to a meeting in a London church was too good to miss, yet as I struggled to get across my conviction that the church must help young people in trouble I was terribly conscious of a man at the back who kept nodding off to sleep. I was astounded when he came to me afterwards and said simply, 'I'll let you have a house rent free so you can start your work here with these kids.'

That night our daily Bible reading was headed with the verse, 'This house will be full with my glory!' We knew it was God's confirmation that we should accept the generous offer.

A month later we watched our few bits and pieces being loaded into a furniture van. What a day that was! The cost of the removal took every penny we could scrape together, yet I felt like Abraham as we prepared for the move to Barnet. Abraham too had known no security as he went into unknown circumstances. He only knew, as I did, that God had said 'go'.

2

It was November, and already dark by the time the removal van was unloaded and we surveyed our new home. I managed to find a corner shop open and bought a small bag of coal. I made up a fire, which spluttered and smoked in the damp fireplace in the living-room of this cold, empty house, and that night we camped down as well as we could. At first light we were up and sorting the precarious heaps of furniture and cardboard boxes that crammed the length of the hall, while Christina crawled from room to room looking puzzled. So we were in London. The trouble was, London did not want to know!

It was difficult not to feel increasingly disappointed as in the days that followed we often knew what it was to be cold and hungry. All the time I was trying to make contact with people who could tell me about the drug problem. I talked with JPs, headmasters and youth club leaders around London, but no one could tell me anything. I visited clubs and coffee bars, talking casually to young people trying to get a 'lead' – but everything seemed to be a dead end.

The Christmas of that first year in London threatened to be a miserable occasion. A friend sent us a chicken, but that was the only thing in the house to remind us that this was a time of festivity! At the last minute, though, a friend phoned to invite us to spend Christmas with his family! We were overjoyed and, armed with our chicken, went to spend a happy few days at their home.

The New Year came and went and I had to admit that our move to London had so far proved anything but revolutionary. I still knew no more about the drug problem, and all the contacts I had made seemed fruitless.

Then one day I picked up a newspaper and my attention was caught immediately by an article on addiction. In it a London doctor was claiming that the country's drug problem was growing very seriously. This was my very first encounter with Dr Peter Chapple and I read his views with great interest, little knowing then what an enormous part this man was to play in my future work. Dr Chapple was quoted as saying that he was very disturbed by the way the Government and other authorities were dealing with the drug problem. Many people, he claimed, refused to admit to accept that Britain had a drug problem at all. They could believe it of America or Hong Kong or other far-removed parts of the world, but not of their own country.

This last point seemed to fit in with my own frustrating experiences of the past months. Many I talked to had been openly derisory of my suggestion that there might be a local drug problem, others had flatly denied even the possibility. I sat down immediately and wrote to Dr Chapple explaining who I was and asking for a meeting with him.

Three days later an official-looking envelope arrived in the post. It was not the expected reply from Dr Chapple but an invitation from the secretary of a large church in Bradford to preach there and meet their elders with a view to becoming the pastor of the church.

This new development was unsettling. It was an honour to be considered for this position, and although Shirley was doubtful the idea was attractive to me.

'Dear Lord,' I prayed as a few weeks later I set off to Bradford, 'if you are calling me to be the pastor of this church, please give me a clear sign.'

After the service that evening one of the elders spoke to me.

'Well, lad, this ought to prove to you that God wants you here.'

I nodded, looking at the crowd of people who had come forward for counselling as I appealed for them to become Christians. Now, an hour later, the building was at last beginning to empty.

So I was almost convinced that this was to be my place – but then a door opened and a young man came in.

That was when I met Michael, the lad with whom this story began; the drug addict whose arrival made me realise that my work was to be not with the large northern church but back in London, with the many, many others like him. That was when I prayed, send me to the Michaels, Lord. Send me to the Michaels.

That boy's salvation confirmed my belief that God alone had the answer to the drug addict's need. Back in London I began to learn more of that need from Dr Chapple, whom I soon came to know and respect deeply. With him I toured hospital wards, encountering cases like Gary, eighteen, who just wanted to be left alone to die, and Phil and Linda, a married couple with no love, no companionship, just a shared craving for the drugs which threatened to destroy them.

Over the weeks that followed I went more and more frequently to the hospital, gradually becoming accepted by the staff and patients. As I entered the building each time I would ask Jesus to come with me, and as I walked those drab corridors and saw so many heart-breaking cases I was aware of his presence and strength.

At night I often walked the streets of Soho and the West end, making contact with young people. The most disturbing thing for me was the emergence of a whole new generation of rebellious youngsters, the drifters. The gangs of earlier days had been based in their areas and formed their own 'patch'. But in the early 1960s many of the young people I began to meet were very far from home. Often they were very young and had left home following some breakdown in relationships within the family. They were sad-faced, forlorn, disillusioned. I used to take one or two home with me and Shirley would cook them a meal. Some took drugs, mainly cannabis, methedrine and amphetamines, and from them I would learn the size of the problems outside the hospital walls.

I gradually learned the places to go where I would be most likely to meet addicts. Whole groups of them would hang around or sleep overnight in toilets. I would go down into many public toilets in the West End to find every cubicle occupied with addicts injecting themselves or homosexuals cohabiting. As I talked to them addicts would glue or Sellotape a hypodermic needle to the end of a glass eyedropper and rubber bulb to inject their drugs, spreading all kinds of diseases as they passed it from one to another. Many had horrible skin complaints and boils and they were thin and weak from malnutrition. Innocent young people attracted on to the fringe of these groups soon became prey to the drug-pushers or homosexuals – or both.

Through my work on the streets and in the hospitals, visiting prisons and courtrooms, I made valuable contacts with social workers, psychiatrists, policemen in the drug squad and others professionally involved with the drug problem.

A year later, almost to the day when I had led Michael to know Christ, I was again in Bradford. I had kept my promise in writing to Michael, but I had not been able to visit him as often as I would have liked to. But he was making his own individual mark in the church youth meetings and was greatly loved. He had introduced several new young people to the church.

All the same, I was haunted by the need for a home for addicts every time I thought of Michael. We had discussed the idea of him moving to London so that I could give him more constant help and advice, but he was understandably frightened that in London the temptation to go back to the old places and get drugs would prove too strong for him. But even in Bradford he seemed so vulnerable and although he was popular he did not have a particularly close friend.

As I prepared for the sermon I was to give at the church that morning I found myself thinking of the last time I had seen Michael. About four months previously as I was travelling through Bradford we had arranged a brief meeting in a coffee bar in the town centre. As he walked in his face was beaming and he was full of excitement.

'Can you imagine it, Frank! I've been accepted to play for a rugby team. Me, a beat-up junkie.'

But Michael wasn't at the service.

21

'That's funny,' said one of the elders, as I stopped him in the porch. 'Well, come to think of it, we haven't seen the lad for three, no, maybe four weeks.'

I was upset, almost angry. I stopped a young man as he was leaving the car park.

'Michael? Yes, that's right, he hasn't been to a service for a few weeks. Wait a minute, though, wasn't there something about him moving to new digs? Yes, that was it. He'll be going somewhere else for fellowship, perhaps. We always remember him in the prayer meeting.'

I was tempted to say something cynical at his last remark, but fought back the words and tried to remain calm. But I was full of apprehension. I began to do a bit of detective work and traced the address of Michael's lodgings – and the telephone number.

The woman's voice was slow, lazy.

'Michael?'

'Yes, Michael Ross.'

'Oh, Mr Ross. Yes, he was one of my gentlemen. Nice boy. But if it's 'is room you want, it's gone. I'm afraid, been taken. Well, you must have heard?'

'Heard what?'

'About Mr Ross. 'E's dead.'

Pain pierced me like an arrow. I stared at the telephone receiver with distaste, an ugly bitterness growing like a lead weight in my stomach.

' 'Ello. 'Ello, dear. You still there?'

This couldn't be my Mr Ross. There had to be some mistake. Not Michael, not my young rugby player.

'Are you sure – about Michael?'

'Well, we all read about it in the evening paper.'

'You read about it? But didn't you say he was staying with you?'

'Well, he was, till three weeks ago. Then he just disappeared, like. In the paper it said he died at Bingley. It must have been him.'

I got into the car and headed for Bingley, a little village just outside Bradford. Disbelief and horror crowded my mind. Michael was the first and only addict I'd helped to start a new life with Jesus. No, he couldn't be dead. It wasn't fair. God wouldn't allow it. Would he?

The constable on duty at Bingley police station was suspicious. I wasn't a relative, so he could tell me nothing. Finally, getting more and more desperate I resorted to name-dropping.

'Look, just give Chief Inspector Spear a ring at the Dangerous Drugs Department of the Home Office. He knows me well and he'll confirm that I really am a worker among addicts and he'll quite likely remember me telling him all about how I was about to help someone called Michael Ross.'

It worked! Apologetically I was ushered into another room, where a second constable sat writing at a desk. After a few more questions about what I knew of Michael they confirmed that a young man had been found dead and identified as a Michael James Ross.

'Cause of death involved an overdose of drugs, sir, so that seems to confirm that it's the young man you knew.'

I was shattered, confused. The police had managed to piece together a probable story from the evidence of a few others he'd been with in a house in Bingley on that particular night. They were old friends of his who had come from Leeds and invited him to a party. Apparently he had been persuaded to take some drugs and had then taken a bath. He had been overcome by the amount of drugs and drowned.

One of the policemen took a file from his desk drawer. Out spilled a sheaf of glossy photographs. They showed

23

a pale thin body lying crumpled up in a bath. It was Michael, all right. There could be no doubts now. Suddenly any further questions seemed irrelevant, and I couldn't wait to get away from the police station.

Lord God, I kept asking, why did this happen? What went wrong? I knew God couldn't fail. So, was it me? I must have failed Michael. I wasn't there when he needed me, even when I'd known deep down inside he needed someone to be near and to care. I should have been there when he needed me this time.

I sat in the car and sobbed. Dear Lord, I prayed, with your help I'll make sure this doesn't happen again. I'll try to be there next time.

For weeks afterwards I spent long hours thinking about a house, a home where I could take in these lost young people and show them Jesus by caring for them and sharing with them all I had.

At the hospital I was learning to work alongside doctors and psychiatrists and to be accepted by them. Gradually hospital staff would involve me in discussions and I grew bold enough to venture a few suggestions. But most of the time I would have to fit into the routine of the hospital day and try not to get in the way.

Much of my time was spent in the occupational therapy room trying to get to know the addict patients by observation and casual conversation. The room was depressing and chilly even in the summer. Patients spent hours there just filling in time, and nothing constructive would go on. Some would daub poster paints around like spoilt nursery children, discarding half-finished scenes of pin men or weird patterns. Others would do some one-finger typing, get frustrated at their mistakes and crash their fists down noisily on the keyboard in disgust. They were bored and difficult to please, like children kept indoors on a rainy day. It seemed impossible for any of them to be creative. They had fallen out of love with the world and needed so much to know the Creator.

Billy, the Canadian addict, would sit in the occupational therapy room for long periods modelling away with slippery lumps of grey clay. I would watch him repeat the same procedure each time. He pummelled away at the clay until a shape would begin to emerge, but just before you could be sure what it was going to be he would always crumple it up with a frown and start again. Whatever he was aiming for, he could never be satisfied with the way it was going. Superficially he was a cheerful boy. His quick jokes and smiles often kept others going when they were feeling rough. But for all that the misery of his own life would often show through and I would shudder at the seeming hopelessness of his case. England had attracted him as a drug haven, but the drugs he had been prescribed free had imprisoned him both physically and spiritually.

One day as I walked into the ward I was amazed to see Billy rushing towards me.

'Hey, Rev,' he shouted, a big grin on his face. 'This Jesus you talk about sure is some kind of guy.'

He began to laugh and waved a Gideon New Testament in front of my face. He seemed to be enjoying some kind of private joke and I wondered if it was going to be at my expense. We sat down together and I asked Billy what he meant.

'Well,' he said, 'I've been reading this story about Jesus and those demons that were in that man, what's 'is name?'

He thumbed through the New Testament and then spread it open on the table.

'Here it is. Legion, that was it. But what a guy that

Jesus was, what a joker! He made all the demons go into the pigs and all the farmers lost their pigs – they drowned themselves in a lake!'

It dawned on me that Billy wasn't leading me on. He was genuinely fascinated by what he considered was Christ's sense of humour!

It was difficult to know what to say. Billy propped his head on his arm and stared at the pages, still giggling. Was this some sort of cry for help? Was this Billy's reluctant way of saying that he was interested in Jesus? Even after these long months of visiting the addict wards not one had ever shown any desire to talk about him.

'Billy,' I faltered, 'Billy, it's possible, you know, to know this Jesus for yourself.'

As soon as the words were out I wished them unsaid. They sounded unreal, cold. How useless I felt, how blind. Billy's laughter was no more than part of his front, his outward face. Inside he was so very sad and broken. How could he possibly want to know Jesus unless a miracle was begun in his heart?

Billy looked at me and I knew our conversation was over. With one last bitter laugh at the pages he jumped up from the table and was gone. I was angry with myself for being so insensitive.

Billy and I had a few more conversations in the weeks that followed, but we never talked about Jesus again, except that sometimes I would hear him say some sort of secret aside: 'That Jesus, what a great guy!'

Then one day when I arrived at the hospital Billy wasn't there. The bed he had occupied was neatly made and the bedside cabinet empty. I poked my head round the door of Dr Chapple's office.

'Where's Billy today?' I called out. 'Couldn't see him anywhere. Have you moved him to another bed?'

'Come in, Frank, and take a seat. Bad news I'm afraid. Billy's dead.'

Another young one, old before he had finished being young, was dead before he had begun to live. The news hit me hard and I went home to mourn and to wonder. It was a few days later before I returned to the hospital and one of the occupational therapists told me how Billy had died. He had slipped out of the locked ward one afternoon as visitors were being let in. He had shut himself in a staff bathroom and was not discovered for some hours. He had hanged himself.

When staff went through his few belongings they found a piece of paper screwed up in his locker drawer, on which was written: 'I can't go on alone any longer.' No one will ever know if these were his last desperate words. Had Billy always been alone, I wondered? Wasn't there somewhere a mother, a brother, an old schoolfriend, a teacher who remembered him and cared if he was alive or dead. What had gone wrong that this young man of twenty-six was so dreadfully alone that he couldn't stand the silence any longer? It was the same kind of loneliness I had seen in Michael. Now they were both dead.

The occupational therapist took me over to the little plastic-topped table where Billy had sat for hours working at his clay modelling. His last model still stood there, unfinished and unwanted like all the rest. It was an ugly primitive animal shape. On the base two capital letters had been heavily scored and underlined. ME. It was an ugly incomplete model of an ugly incomplete life. This was what drugs had done. Drugs demand every part of a mind and body. It was futile to shout 'Stop! Stop!' An addict is incapable of stopping by his own strength. He is a prisoner of a cruel master, and only the power of Christ can set him wholly free.

One addict once described his drug experiences to me as being a love affair. He was completely enslaved to his lust for heroin and talked of the snowy white powder and the shining needle that dominated his life in terms of grotesque affection. Another addict asked me: 'What can your Jesus give me that drugs can't? You talk about peace – but there's nothing more peaceful than a trip when drugs take you over. You talk about freedom and an answer to my problems – well, heroin obliterates them. You talk about a life hereafter – well, I've been there already. Heroin has taken me there and back again.' Many addicts are convinced that they have found heaven on drug trips which have given them hallucinations. One young man talked of having a beautiful experience of walking down streets paved with gold.

Phil and Linda would sit for hours strumming an old guitar. Linda talked profusely sometimes, but at others seemed almost not to know me and sat staring wistfully into space. Although Phil had a pretty bad family background Linda's was quite different. Her father was a company director and nothing had been spared to give her a good education. Bitterness and disgust at finding that Linda was addicted to drugs had robbed her parents of every last vestige of concern for her and they had finally disowned her completely.

'Frank, if you'd like to do something really useful . . . ' said Dr Chapple one day. He was wondering if Shirley and I would have Phil and Linda to stay with us for a week-end. So, a little apprehensively, I bundled the couple into the back of my car one Friday afternoon and took them home.

Phil was nervous and spent most of the week-end smoking cigarettes and waiting for the appointed times when I would open the medicine cabinet and let them have their daily doses of physeptone – the maintenance drug prescribed in linctus form at the hospital in gradually decreasing amounts. Linda was soon occupied with the children and got on well with Shirley.

Somehow it seemed much easier to talk about Christian things in our own home than in the cold clinical hospital surroundings. We began to talk to them about our belief that Jesus could give a new and complete freedom to the addict and enable him to live a full life without the prop of drugs. And as we talked Phil and Linda's eyes, at least in some small measure, began to open to spiritual things for the first time, as if they caught a faint glimmer of hope. It was good to be away from the pressures and restrictions of the hospital ward. I realised how great was the spiritual battle I fought at the hospital, where the very atmosphere was charged with opposition in wards where insanity and instabilities of every kind seemed in control.

In talking to that young mixed-up couple, Shirley and I knew that to be really effective in any kind of rehabilitation work we had to take addicts out of the streets of London, away from the places where the temptation to take drugs was simply too great for them to handle. We needed a house – but not just any house. It had to be a sanctuary, a rescue centre, a home far from the harsh reality of all that reminded these young people of their slavery to drugs. A house in the country.

On Monday night I returned Phil and Linda to the hospital and went home to pray with Shirley. 'God, we need a house. A big house, Lord, a house in the country. Not for us but for all the Phils and Lindas, the Michaels, the Billys, and all the hundreds more we want to reach for you.'

That simple prayer, not a fanfare or special loud

announcement, introduced an entirely fresh concept into our ministry. All that had happened so far had somehow crystallised that week-end into a deep conviction that God wanted us to open a home for all these lost young people. From that moment Shirley and I became house hunters for God.

3

One evening Dr Chapple called after me as he opened his car door. I went across and he handed me a letter.

'Here's someone you might like to help. A girl called Jenny Baxter. She's been a patient for some time at my Lambeth clinic. Her letter's a bit confused; she seems to have read some book called *The Cross and the Switchblade*, about some American chap who sounds a bit like you. I don't know if anyone could help the girl, but when she came to the clinic last night, after she'd sent me this letter, I told her a bit about you. She'd like to meet you. I've written her address on the back of the envelope. See what you can do. Good night.'

The car door slammed and he was gone. I walked across to my old Ford, turning the letter slowly in my hand. What a sad and ironic address for a young girl mixed up in drugs. 118 Hope House . . .

All hope seemed to have died for Mrs Baxter.

'Jenny's out. I mean . . . well, I haven't seen her for a few days, but please come in.'

Jenny's mother was a short plump woman with untidy brown and grey hair flopping over her forehead. She smiled at me uncertainly, but it was grief I saw in her eyes immediately. And every line on her face seemed to betray the agony of having a drug addict for a daughter.

The flat, on the fifth floor of a middle-class modern block, was small but tastefully furnished and decorated with a sense of modest prosperity. Mr Baxter was hunched up in a comfortable armchair in the living-room watching the television, which he switched off immediately he saw me come in. He rose to shake hands. Like the flat he was small and neat.

'Tom's in plastics,' said Mrs Baxter, bringing in a tray of coffee and biscuits. Tom nodded shyly.

'Yes,' went on his wife, 'Built up his own little business over the years and now it's doing so well. If it wasn't for Jenny, Mr Wilson, we'd be so happy. But we're at our wits' end, we really are.'

She sat down pensively, smoothing her tweed skirt over her knees.

'Sometimes we think there isn't any hope left for her, and it breaks our hearts. When we first found out about her taking drugs we were so shocked. She was so young, still at school, and now she's twenty-two and her whole life's finished, such a mess. We had a bad car accident, you see, and Jenny was unconscious for a fortnight. Three weeks after that she went kind of mental, you know. Well, we thought it was the accident, naturally. Then the psychiatrist told us she had been taking drugs, and it was the withdrawal effects.

'Never in our wildest dreams did we guess anything like that might happen to one of our two girls. Drugs – well, they were something foreign to us.'

She stood up abruptly and took a little gilt framed picture from the mantelpiece, and pressed it into my hand. An attractive young girl smiled up at me. Was this Jenny?

'Our Sylvia,' said Mrs Baxter. 'Two years older than Jenny. She's married these past eighteen months to such a nice lad. They come and see us for tea nearly every Sunday. Her and Jenny were so close when they were children. We treated them fairly, just the same, and yet now they couldn't be more different.

'We're so proud of Sylvia. Yet Jenny . . . you can't understand what it's like being her mother. She disappears for weeks on end, and then I'm worried sick wondering what's happening to her, wondering if the police are going to ring up one day and say something terrible's happened. And when she comes home it's awful. In such a small flat I know every movement she makes. She locks herself in the bathroom for hours on end. You hear the tinkling noises and you know she's just going to inject herself. I just sit out here and wait till she's finished and go in and clean up after her. There'll be blood on the wall by the sink. Sometimes you tread on needles she didn't know she'd dropped, she's so out of her mind with the drugs. We've pleaded with her for hours but she just sits there, like a stranger, cold and far away. We've done all we can, haven't we, Tom?'

I noticed Mr Baxter again, nodding silently in his chair in the corner of the room. He sat with his head propped on his hands, his eyes downward. His broken attitude of hopelessness was perhaps even more expressive of grief than his wife's more obvious distress, and my heart went out to him.

'It's that Tony, for one thing,' said Mr Baxter, slowly.

'Tony?' I asked.

'Yes, Tony,' said Mrs Baxter. 'Some kind of boy friend she stays with off and on. He's an addict, too. When Jenny used to bring young men home we always used to think maybe this one will be a nice boy with a steady job and they'll get married and she'll stop all her wild ways. But every one that's come in makes our hearts sink. They'd be awful rough boys some of them, with long hair and filthy jeans. And they'd be taking drugs, too. And Tony, he's the worst of them all. Oh, he can look a bit smarter than the rest. He's got some fancy clothes, but he's a crook. I won't have him in the house now. Sometimes when we've taken Jenny away with us for a few weeks she'd be improving a bit, and she'd cut down on the drugs. Then when we came home again Tony would turn up on the doorstep and she'd be off like a shot, running after him like he was the Pied Piper. We even saved up enough money to send her to South Africa last year, to stay for a month with some relatives. When she came back she looked much brighter, but then just two days later and there was a knock at the door. It was Tony, and she was gone within five minutes.'

We talked together for a long time that evening. Mrs Baxter seemed relieved at being able to talk to someone about Jenny and I promised I would keep in touch with them, try to trace Jenny, and do all I could to help. But coming away from Hope House I took away with me some of their despair and hopelessness. I tossed and turned all night, wondering what I could do to help Jenny. But not just Jenny – and to help Mr and Mrs Baxter too. They were good decent people. They loved Jenny, even now. So often parents and home background are pointed to as underlying causes for a young person turning to drugs. But the same excuse could not be made for Jenny. She had had as many good chances in life as her sister,

Sylvia. Her parents' anguish kept coming back to me and I felt helpless. I saw the bowed head of Mr Baxter as he sat quietly in his corner chair. I saw the tears that filled Mrs Baxter's eyes as she sat awkwardly twisting her handkerchief between her fingers. Could I say that they'd done anything wrong for Jenny?

I couldn't sleep. Finally I left the bedroom and crept downstairs to the little front room I used as my study. Fragments of Bible verses kept coming to me and I had to look them up. I found them in the book of Isaiah, a passage in chapter 61 which foretold the ministry of Jesus.

> The Spirit of the Lord God is upon me; because the Lord hath anointed me to preach good tidings unto the meek; he hath sent me to bind up the brokenhearted, to proclaim liberty to the captives, and the opening of the prison to them that are bound; to proclaim the acceptable year of the Lord, and the day of vengeance of our God; to comfort all that mourn; to appoint unto them that mourn in Zion, to give unto them beauty for ashes, the oil of joy for mourning, the garment of praise for the spirit of heaviness; that they might be called trees of righteousness, the planting of the Lord, that he might be glorified.

I fed on these words and found hope again. I knew even in this dark situation God would bring light, and I prayed that he would use me to do it.

The next day we had a letter from our landlord. Due to personal difficulties he had no alternative but to sell the house which he had given us to live in rent free for what was almost a year. What was the next step? Somehow this new problem didn't fill me with apprehension. We'd walked this road before. I had learned that God was leading us and was confident in the provision of a new home.

Days were nothing but hard, but wonderfully jig-sawed together to make a marvellous training programme for me – a carefully detailed preparation for the future of which at that time I only dreamed. As I walked the lamplit streets of the West End, as I struggled for words sitting by the hospital bedside of a hardened heroin addict, and in the very real personal and domestic problems of the everyday – in everything I was aware of God the Teacher. He was alongside me, pointing out the lessons. He was lending me some of his great wisdom and I was learning. I was learning about trusting him, about the heartbreak of young addicts, about the agony of parents like the Baxters, about the helplessness and heart-searching of the doctor, about the limitations of the law.

I put the landlord's letter aside and reached for the phone. Mrs Baxter had given me the address of Jenny's doctor. His home and surgery in Islington were Jenny's supply line of drugs, and I knew that she would be maintaining contact with him. I explained who I was, and I was warmly invited to visit him one evening the following week.

The tall, narrow Victorian house I found myself in was gaunt and sombre, set in a whole row of identically depressing houses, some boarded up for demolition.

'Jenny Baxter is in many ways a typical example of the classic drug taker,' said the doctor, showing me into his clean and comfortable surgery. 'She lives for her drugs and nothing else seems to matter to her at all. She's completely lost her self respect, and the normal claims of society and family don't touch her at all.'

The doctor was small and dark. Italian, I guessed, though it was hard to tell as his English was almost faultless. He took out a sheaf of notes from a filing tray and led me into a little living-room at the back of the house. He spread out Jenny's case notes on the green velvety cloth on an old table near the window and left me to read through them while he made some coffee.

The coffee was dark and bitter. The doctor began to describe the hopelessness of his young girl patient. He had tried to cut down her drugs but she had resorted to supplementing her dose by theft, so now he had given up. At least, he said, she knew she could get drugs from him and so he was in contact and might at some future date be able to wean her from them. I asked about the mystical Tony. Did he know where Jenny and Tony were now?

'Probably at the Savoy, for all I know,' said the doctor with a laugh.

I looked puzzled and he went on to explain.

'Only the best hotels,' he said. 'Jenny and Tony are expert at foiling desk clerks. They keep one set of good clothes each, and book into an hotel giving the impression of being a young businessman and his wife. Tony's got plenty of stolen American Express travellers' cards and other reference papers. They live it up at the hotel for as long as they think they can bluff it out and then disappear one night. Then it's back to living rough till the heat dies down, and on to another unsuspecting hotel.

'I don't know where they are at the moment. Jenny's not very good at keeping appointments but she's quick to come round when she needs more drugs. I'll see if I can get her to come in after surgery hours one night and give you a ring. But you'll have to be prepared for the possibility of her not turning up. But, then, if she told Dr Chapple she wanted to meet you, I'll do all I can to arrange it.'

On the way home from the Islington surgery I called in

on the Baxters to let them know I'd been to see Jenny's doctor and was hopeful I'd be able to meet their daughter soon.

'Oh, Mr Wilson, if only you'd called last night!' said a distraught Mrs Baxter as she opened the door to me.

Jenny had apparently turned up there in the middle of the evening.

'It was the first time we'd seen her for weeks, and all she wanted was some money. I did try to be a bit hard on her, but it was like sticking a knife in myself. Dad told her straight. "I refuse to let you go on tormenting your mother any more," he said. It is torment, really it is. Well, there was a dreadful scene. She took some things from her room and said she was going to sell them to get some money. Dad tried to talk some sense into her, but honestly it's like knocking your head against a brick wall. Sometimes she just seems like a vegetable. It's a nightmare. I keep hoping I'm going to wake up and find my two little girls again, both as right as ninepence. Jenny's with me all the time. She's never out of my thoughts, haunting me.'

With a hopeless shrug of her shoulders Mrs Baxter sank on to the settee in the lounge. Mr Baxter came over and awkwardly put his arms round his wife's shoulders. It was hard to know what to say to them.

It was almost two weeks later when the doctor rang to say that Jenny was coming to see him that evening. He hadn't mentioned me to her, but thought it would be all right if I turned up and he would introduce me.

Jenny was late. The doctor invited me to take a chair in the corner of his surgery and apologetically carried on with some paperwork. Half an hour passed. An hour. Finally there was a knock at the door. Jenny followed the doctor into the surgery and, completely ignoring me, slumped into the chair across the desk from him. She

38

fumbled in her pockets, took out a packet of cigarettes and lit one. She drew deeply and sighed, watching the doctor listlessly as he took his prescription pad and began to fill it in.

The dark hair and dark eyes were reminiscent of the attractive young woman in the gilt framed picture on the Baxters' mantelpiece – the happily married Sylvia. But there the similarity ended. Jenny's skin was pale and blotchy with bluish marks. Her eyelids were dark and heavy, her eyes dull, her long hair unwashed and uncombed. She was wearing old jeans and dirty shapeless grey jumper, with a ragged multicoloured silk scarf tied round her neck. She had a large bulging canvas bag with her.

Drugs seemed to have robbed Mrs Baxter of her motherhood in depriving her of any workable relationship with her daughter. I could see now that drugs had robbed Jenny of her femininity, her youth and her beauty. She had the haunted, lonely look of the junkie.

'Here you are, Jenny.'

She grabbed the prescription from the doctor's outstretched hand and scanned it hungrily.

'Look, Doc, can't you put more on this script. I need more than that. Please, Doc?'

For the next five minutes Jenny did her best to convince the doctor that if he didn't prescribe her more heroin she would be on the threshold of death. The doctor grimly held his ground, and finally she subsided.

'Well, have you put some new needles on?'

'Yes, Jenny. But remember – I've given you just enough for yourself. Don't give any away to Tony.'

'Oh, I haven't seen him for ages.'

The conversation continued, now a little more friendly. The doctor asked where she was living, what she was managing to get to eat. Her answers were vague and suggested the total disorder of her life. She began to fidget on the edge of her seat, eager to get away and get her prescription turned into drugs at the all night chemist. I was amazed that she continued to be apparently completely oblivious to my presence.

'One more thing, Jenny,' said the doctor. 'Remember asking Dr Chapple about someone called Frank Wilson?'

'Wilson? Oh, yes, I guess so. I wrote a letter.'

'Well, Mr Wilson's come along tonight to meet you,' he said, nodding towards me in the corner.

Jenny's nonchalance evaporated. She swivelled round in her chair to face me.

'Oh God! I'm sorry. You! I wanted it to be different. I mean, I really wanted to meet you in a different way.'

'Well, Jenny,' I said, 'perhaps this really was the best way for me to get to know you.'

I found conversation with her difficult. After a while I wondered how I could bring everything to a close. Jenny was getting really anxious to go, and I felt it would be better to meet her again under different circumstances.

'My wife and I would love you to come and stay with us some time, Jenny,' I said, getting up from my chair.

The doctor stood up too. 'Yes, why don't you do that, Jenny? You say you want to help, and Mr Wilson wants to learn how he could best help young people like you. You could help each other out, in a way.'

Jenny looked up at me. Her initial embarrassment had gone, and now she was the hard junkie again, sizing me up.

'Well,' she said, 'I've got nowhere to go tonight . . .'

Not quite sure how I'd got myself into the situation, I found myself driving home ten minutes later with a passenger. We stopped at the chemist for Jenny to pick up her drugs. What would Shirley think I wondered as we drew up outside the house. I realised that there was another car outside our home and recognised it as belonging to an old friend of ours – Bill Thompson, a member of a Christian businessmen's organisation. Now it was my turn to be embarrassed as I introduced Jenny to both Shirley and Bill. Jenny unceremoniously dropped into the nearest armchair as if she owned the place.

At first opportunity I followed Shirley out to the kitchen where she was making coffee, and explained as briefly as I could about Jenny's unexpected arrival. I needn't have worried. Shirley was pleased to have an opportunity of helping this young addict.

'Frank,' she said, 'what do you think? Mr Thompson thinks he's got an answer to our accommodation problem.'

I had almost forgotten that we were very shortly to be faced with the problem of homelessness.

'He says he and his wife have a very big house and he's offered us rooms in it to stay in.'

There was no chance to discuss this, and anyway Jenny was my first consideration. Mr Thompson did not stay long. As soon as he was gone Jenny said: 'Do you mind if I use your bathroom?'

I was a little wary. I remembered her mother's description of her use of the bathroom.

'What for?' I asked.

She gave me a mouthful of abuse, explaining she only wanted to use the toilet.

'Are you sure you don't want to have a fix?' I asked.

She hung her head.

'I've got Shirley and the children to think of, Jenny. You can use the front room.'

I took Jenny into the little barely furnished front room which doubled as a storeroom and study. I swept some papers off my desk and sat her down. She was shaking. She asked me for matches, a glass of water and a spoon, which I fetched from the kitchen. She began to heat the little white heroin pills and water in a spoon over the flame of a match. Quickly she drew the liquid into her syringe and wrapped her coloured scarf around her arm to form a tourniquet. She began to hunt for a raised vein along her scarred arms.

Right then, as I watched this deadly ritual, it was difficult not to feel utterly nauseated. She plunged the needle into her vein and two or three times drew up her own blood into the syringe and pumped it back into her arm till every trace of heroin was gone. I wanted to cry out to her to stop, or to physically restrain her, but I knew that wasn't the answer. She was destroying herself and hadn't the will to do anything else.

Jenny wiped the needle on her scarf and put all her equipment away in a little plastic cosmetics bag. Already her eyes were glazing over and her tense body was beginning to relax. I left her and went back to the living-room. I realised now more than ever the slavery of addiction. Jenny was paying homage to a master stronger than herself. The master had taken over her whole body, was claiming her entirely. How long would it be before only death would satisfy him?

A little later Jenny emerged and joined us. She was buoyant and cheerful now and very talkative, 'high' on heroin. She was able to communicate with people now, protected by the cotton wool padding of her drug trip.

Shirley and I began to talk to her about our hopes and plans to open a centre to help people like her. Jenny agreed that she needed help. Somehow it was easier for her to talk about being without drugs now that she had had a fix. She began to tell us all about her life, and about

Tony. And she began to listen, too, as we began to talk to her about our belief that God could help the addict to be completely free from drugs.

At that time I was naïve enough to be encouraged by her enthusiastic response. She convinced us that she really wanted help. Even God's help. Finally she agreed to my suggestion that she should ask God's help to overcome her craving and throw away the rest of her drugs. We flushed the pills away down the toilet and prayed with her. How little we understood then! Shirley and I put her to bed that night really thinking that we had seen a miracle.

The noise of footsteps woke me in the early hours of the morning. I threw on my dressing gown and went out on to the landing. Jenny, dressed and with her dirty canvas bag slung over her shoulder was half-way down the stairs. No amount of talking or arguing or persuading would make her stay. Her need for drugs was too great and all she could think of was how to get more.

'Tony will get me some. Or that stupid doctor.'

Before the sun had risen on a new day Jenny had disappeared into the greyness of the city.

4

A few days later we made the move to the Thompsons'
house in Chingford. We were grateful for their offer. In-
deed, it was the only door open to us. We had nowhere else
to go. But we knew we were facing a difficult situation;
living in someone else's home, sharing their bathroom and
kitchen. Once again we realised the difficulties of the work
we had taken on. We had to be prepared to be uncertain
of the future, to rest in knowing that our confidence and
security came from something far greater than the things
around us.

I continued my regular visits to the hospital and work
on the streets. As I learned more about the tragedy of the
addict my own future became clearer. I was more and
more certain of the need for a large house, a rehabilitation
centre out in the country. And if I was to begin this kind
of work I knew I needed to be working on some sort of
structure. I had come to know several Christian people
who were keenly interested in my work and wanted to
support me, and I began to gather together the nucleus of

44

a yet uncreated organisation, with Bill Thompson as its chairman. Our little group met together in his house to pray and plan.

Three or four weeks after we had moved to Chingford I had a surprise telephone call from Jenny one evening. I had heard nothing from her since that eventful night when she stayed with us, but I had contacted her doctor and left our new address and telephone number with him.

'I'm in trouble,' said Jenny.

She was in a little pub in the West End, ringing from a booth in the ladies' cloakroom. There was a big man after her, a 'giant', she said, and he wanted to sexually assault her.

I was sceptical. Was she really in trouble or was this just some attention-drawing fantasy?

She began to cry. 'Frank, please help me. I'm scared.'

I drove off to the West End and found the little pub. Awkwardly, I asked the barmaid if she would look in the cloakroom for me, as I thought a young woman I knew might be waiting for me there. She gave me a withering look and went off. But she came back shaking her head. 'Sorry,' she said. 'Your friend must have stood you up.'

Embarrassed, I made for the door. Then in a corner of the pub I spotted Rob, a young addict I had met several times in the West End. I went over and talked to him and his group of friends for a few minutes before leaving. Jenny or no Jenny, I thought, it had been worth the journey just to meet Rob, and continue my contact with him.

Outside I turned up my collar and shivered. A figure stepped out of the shadows and I jumped. It was Jenny.

'Oh, here you are at last!' She sounded exasperated. I opened the car door and she slumped into the passenger seat.

'Well, young woman,' I said, 'what's your explanation for all this?'

Her story gradually emerged. She had 'conned' some money from some unsuspecting man by making him think she was a prostitute. However, she didn't plan her get-away very well, and the man, realising he had been tricked, followed her to the pub and demanded his money back. Jenny had disappeared into the cloakroom, where she had phoned me. A little later she had climbed out through the toilet window.

'And all because of him I've missed Tony,' she moaned. 'We'd arranged to meet at nine and it's gone ten now. I knew he wouldn't wait for me, Frank, do you think you could give me a lift?'

She named a street off Trafalgar Square where I knew crowds of addicts hung out most evenings.

'Okay, Jenny. But only if you'll introduce me to a few of your friends.'

She agreed. Jenny, I realised, was a pass key into a world to which I couldn't gain entrance very easily. With her by my side I would be much more readily accepted by other addicts.

Jenny, half hoping I would give her some money to 'score' some drugs, casually introduced me to some of her friends. I had learned enough of the scene to identify them by now. There were the clusters of young lesbian girls and homosexual boys waiting on the corners to be picked up by older homosexuals. Many of them were addicts and had been forced to sell their bodies in this way to get money for drugs. There were the usual gypsy types and filthy old tramps, but somehow the young people on those streets were much more tragic. Some had only been looking for enjoyment, for more to life than they had. They had foolishly been deceived by the attractive promises of drugs. The anguish on their faces was only matched by the anguish I saw during my hospital visits. This truly was 'heartbreak corner'.

In the weeks that followed this incident I met up with Jenny again several times and tried to talk to her about giving up drugs and going home. Sometimes she would be agreeing with me and ready to go into hospital for a medical withdrawal from drugs. But by the time of the next fix she had changed her mind. Like most addicts she insisted she was in control of her drugs and could give up when she wanted to. We walked the streets together and sat in dingy coffee bars. When the theatres and cinemas closed their doors and the restaurants had served their last meal a whole underworld emerged, and, with Jenny again as my pass-key, I would be able to approach many young people and talk to them. Often I felt like giving up. There seemed to be no result. But I knew that I was building up relationships with these young people which might later mean a whole new life. If only one came through it would have been worth it all.

One boy I often talked to was Danny, just fifteen years old, although he looked much older. He smelt vile and his face was covered with sores as a result of his general uncleanliness and his habit of using dirty needles to inject himself. He was as thin as a rake. Somewhere in his past was a mother and father, a home and a warm bed, but something he could hardly account for prevented him from going back. He had joined the great movement of young people that was turning away from convention and the tried and tested. He despised security and materialism. I would sit on the pavement talking to him. Go back to his parents? They led such miserable humdrum narrow lives, he said. I sighed as I looked at him. Was his life really any different? I never saw him smile.

47

His world was the walk from the chemist to the public lavatory, his home the gutter.

Another I often met was Duffy, an addict who worked in the evenings as a bouncer in an awful back street pub. Among the loud-mouthed brawlers I would often find little sad-faced groups of addicts at this pub, slip into their circle and listen to their conversation. They all seemed, like Danny, to despise their parents' respectability, and thought they had actually achieved something good by walking out on them.

As I got to know them I would venture to challenge them. 'Look,' I would say, 'you all think you've got freedom. But like your parents you've got your own conventions. You've got your own little culture. You all wear the same clothes. You all even speak your own language. You all think there is something to be gained by not working. You think you're paying back society for a bad deal. Are you really any different from your parents?'

The most I seemed to be able to give to many of these young people was my friendship, a cup of coffee or a meal. But always I realised that their greatest need was for a personal experience with Jesus Christ, for God to revolutionise their lives. Addicts need a reason to live without drugs. Medical care could offer no worthwhile reason – my visits to the hospital confirmed that. Time after time I would see the admission of a young boy or girl who had been released only months before as 'cured'. Outside the hospital they would come face to face with the same temptations to take drugs. They would walk the same streets where they met pushers. They would walk into pubs and meet their old friends taking drugs. After a short time even the strongest willed would give in. They had no good reason not to. It was even accepted as normal that an addict patient would return to his old life, the

48

old culture, and succumb within quite a short time to the pull of drugs. The doctors showed no surprise when familiar faces turned up in the casualty department or when 'cured' patients were brought in on stretchers after being picked up from the gutters of a Soho street, unconscious from an overdose.

Phil and Linda, the married couple I regularly visited at Dr Chapple's clinic, were discharged and went to live in a flat in Hampstead. I decided to go and visit them one evening. The front door of the large house was ajar so I pushed it open and walked inside. I knocked timidly on the first door, found myself confronted with a very formidable looking landlady. I asked if I could see Phil and Linda.

'Oh, them two! They're not in very much, I can tell you. Shouldn't be at all surprised if they're out tonight. And when they are in there's a lot of noise all the time from their so-called friends. Drunks I call 'em. Can't get a minute's peace in me own house. And they're three weeks behind with their rent.'

She looked at me expectantly, almost as if she was waiting for me to take out my wallet and nobly pay the rent bill. I asked if I could wait for them or leave a note, and she begrudgingly showed me up to a top floor flat and pushed the door open for me.

The room was in a terrible state. It was just a one-room flat with a curtained off wash area at one end. The trappings of the junkie were strewn everywhere – discarded matches, empty ampoules and syringes on the bed and scattered on the floor. The sink was full of dirty dishes. There was a bookcase full of pornographic paperbacks.

I waited for a while, and then decided the best thing was to leave a note, so I scribbled a hasty letter on the back of an old envelope and left it propped up against an ashtray on the chest of drawers near the bed. I let myself out quietly, dodging the landlady.

It was soon after this that I stumbled across quite a big drug-taking ring operating from a big house in the Victoria area. I first heard about it from an eighteen-year-old called Dave. Dave told me he had started on drugs when he was persuaded to try a fix of heroin at a week-end party in this particular house. He had been invited back each week-end and was given heroin each time. After only a couple of months he realised he was physically dependent on the drug, but the next time he went along to the house he was turned away and told to go and get registered. Jenny also gave me information about this group. It seemed that just a handful of them seemed bent on making as many young people as possible into addicts. The leader, I discovered, was a young man called Mike Coombes and he was aided and abetted by his girlfriend and a couple of friends.

For all the evil and rottenness I recognised in what Mike Coombes was doing to so many young people, I realised that he, too, was a victim of his own foolishness and slavery to drugs. I asked Jenny if she could arrange some way for me to visit Mike and after a few weeks she told me she'd take me round to see him the following Saturday.

However, I was too late. Mike was arrested just two days before I was to see him. After finding various drug charges against him proved the court sentenced Mike to six months in prison. I heard that, being deprived for some reason of the proper medication to withdraw from drugs, Mike endured several days of physical agony going through 'cold turkey'. One morning, unable to take any more, he had hung himself from the prison cell door with his belt.

I knew that the London prisons had many addicts as prisoners and Mike's death, although I had never met him, made me decide to try to help these if I could. I wrote to the prison authorities asking if I could visit addicts in prison. The official reply stated that prisoners were adequately catered for by the prison chaplaincy and that there was no need for me to visit them. I wrote back immediately saying that I didn't consider that the spiritual care offered to prisoners was so good in view of the fact that one I knew had killed himself.

There were more letters, and finally I was given permission to go into prisons to visit addicts I knew who had found their way there. And so I was able to expand my contact with addicts in yet one more direction.

Now we were nearer to finding our house for God than we knew. First Bill Thompson and some friends set up a home for addicts at Tournours Hall, near London, but that, God made it clear, was not for me. With Shirley, always encouraging, helpful, loving, I faced the prospect of imminent homelessness once more, and waited, trusting God.

The next step was a three-months stay in Kent at the home of some fine Christian friends, Dr and Mrs Claxton. Here, with the help of a group of other friends, our organisation for the rescuing of drug addicts took a definite form. We became an official body, with the name Life for the World. It was very exciting.

Something important had been born. We weren't on our own any more. Life for the World collected its own little band of voluntary workers who came in to help me in a little makeshift office in Dr Claxton's house, typing letters and sending out duplicated newsletters to a handful of supporters. Contacts I had made over the previous few years began to emerge as more than faces in a crowd – they became friends who stood alongside me and began to understand and care about young addicts.

Gordon Hunt was one of these, a Baptist minister who was the pastor of a church in St Leonards, Hastings. From time to time I had been invited to speak to his church members at their revival prayer meetings, and it was on one of these occasions that Gordon announced that the church had put some money together to buy me a car. I was overwhelmed by the way in which these people expressed their genuine care for me and their support for what I was trying to do.

Their caring made a deep impression on me. As I drove away in my newly acquired Vauxhall Victor Estate I remember thinking that this was the kind of church, these were the kind of people, I would want a young addict to belong to, to really receive practical and spiritual support to enable him to live free of the prop of drugs and become a useful alive member of society.

Some time later this 'dream' was put to the test when I came into contact with John and Jackie Blake, a young married couple seriously addicted to hard drugs.

I met John Blake in his mother's flat in a soaring new block built on the site of the demolished East End slums. As I walked in through the entrance I saw both lifts standing open – obviously out of order. Glass from the doors lay in splinters on the floor. The lifts stank of urine and were littered with screwed up drinks cartons and newspapers. I climbed the weary concrete steps to the ninth floor. The walls were scrawled with graffiti and on every landing I recognised what had been little indoor gardens – ornate pedestals and pots for shrubs and plants – wrecked and covered with rubbish of all descriptions.

I realised how little slums had to do with buildings – slums were about people, not bricks and mortar. The

52

hopeful replacing of the slum streets by these modern skyscrapers had just produced a different kind of horror. Changing the environment had not changed the people. Was it any wonder that kids were looking for an escape from distasteful reality and turning to the 'kicks' of the drug scene?

I had been asked to see John and Jackie by an East End clergyman who had tried unsuccessfully to help them. This couple, in their late twenties, had two young children, now in the care of the local authority. Jackie was in hospital following a heavy drug overdose and John was staying with his mother.

John had the tired eyes of the confirmed junkie, but in other ways did not look the typical dropout. His dark hair was short, he was casually but neatly dressed. He was quiet and withdrawn and would say little to me, just that he was a jazz singer and had a heavy heroin habit. But he did tell me which hospital Jackie was in and was willing for me to go and see her.

Jackie was hard. Very hard. It was the same hardness I had seen in many young girl addicts. Somehow they were that much more difficult to reach than the boys; they kept their distance. They had lost their femininity and softness, the essence of their womanhood, in their enslavement to drugs, in a way that the boys and men never suffered with a lack of masculinity. Perhaps it was something to do with the 'tough' image of the junkie that went unnoticed in a man but became ugly in a girl. I had seen all this in Jenny, and was seeing it again in the young white-faced woman lying in the hospital bed. She was hard, and yet now and again I could detect a hint of a lost someone crying out to be loved, especially when she spoke about her two children, a boy of five and a girl of three.

Jackie was in a single room on a drip feed. Like her

husband she was addicted to heroin, but she had taken an overdose of barbiturates and had been given stomach pump treatment. Her pale face was contrasted by her short gingery hair. She had a deep husky voice with a strong accent which I later realised was the Channel Islands accent. One side of her family was French and her home was Guernsey, or had been till she had left home in search of adventure.

There was no problem getting Jackie to talk, unlike John. It was difficult, though, to separate fact from fiction. She spun me a fairly improbable tale about having seen a vision of Christ when she had been on the point of death, yet I didn't feel I ought to dismiss it as a complete fantasy; it seemed real enough to her. I had often been gullible enough to be taken in by stories of encounters with the supernatural told to me by addicts who knew I was a minister and were hoping to 'con' me out of a few pounds for the next 'fix'.

I wasn't sure about this particular 'vision', but I was sure that she was a desperate young woman whose life was in ruins, and Life for the World should do all it could to help.

Although she had really nothing to offer them – no home, no security of any kind – Jackie was desperate to be reunited with her children. She saw the social services as some kind of evil ogre who had stolen them from her by deception. She begged me to help her get her children back. I promised I would do all I could.

I told Shirley all about John and Jackie and she was so concerned about them that we both sat down to think and pray about how we could help them. They were homeless and we knew something of that heartbreak. Separated from their children, too. We could appreciate that particular agony, at the same time realising that addicts could not by definition be good parents. Their devotion to drugs superseded ties to other people, even very tiny people who needed their parents' love and protection.

It was then that we thought of Gordon Hunt and the loving fellowship of Christians at St Leonards. It was asking a lot of anybody, but we didn't know any other group so well equipped with love. Would they be able to help John and Jackie sort themselves out, get a home, give up drugs and bring up their children?

I phoned Gordon the next day and we arranged to meet to discuss the practical side of this problem. He was certainly enthusiastic about helping John and Jackie and was confident his church members would be in full support.

Meanwhile life was very busy. I was continuing with a very full programme of hospital, clinic and prison visiting, not forgetting the occasional night visit to 'heartbreak corner', the city's underworld of prostitution, petty crime and addiction with which I was becoming so familiar. Yet, though familiar in the sense of my growing knowledge and awareness of the drug scene, I was continually affected by the terrible sadness of it all, and I had to battle against my sense of inadequacy, faced by so many broken lives.

It was about this time that I came in contact with Audrey.

5

I'll never forget my first meeting with Audrey. It started
with a letter from Tooting Bec Mental hospital:

> Dear Rev,
>   I have heard you help drug addicts. I'm told I'm
> beyond help but if you can spare time to say a prayer for
> me I would be grateful.
>   Cheerio!
>
>   Love, Audrey Williams

It was so simple and almost childlike that it prompted my
immediate response, and one week later I climbed the
concrete steps of the grim psychiatric ward at Tooting
where Audrey was locked away with all kinds of mentally
ill and insane people, plus a few other female addicts.

I had written to her and, not knowing really how to say
what I felt, I had replied in much the same simple manner
as Audrey had written. I said ' . . . don't give up hope,
even if others have, there really is an answer and I will

come and see you and tell you all about it!' I wondered what response my letter received and what kind of reception I would get as I pressed the polished brass bell push outside the locked ward.

The busy little nurse who opened the door, directed me towards the hive of activity going on around the television set in the smoke-filled part of the ward which they called the sitting-room. The ward was typical of so many I had visited, grim, smelly and depressing. A few pictures hung at an odd angle on the dark yellow walls and the view through the few windows was obscured by London dirt and wire mesh.

At first everyone ignored me. A heated discussion was going on about the merits or lack of them of a TV star who was vainly singing his heart out on the seventeen inch screen. Then, a small elderly lady in carpet slippers and a flowered pattern frock walked up to me, a cigarette hanging from toothless lips.

' 'Ello dearie!' she said peering up at me. 'Ain't you a big boy!'

I tried to maintain my ministerial composure.

'Oh, can you help me; I'm trying to find Audrey Williams?'

She ignored the question.

' 'Ere luv, 'ave you got a fag for an old lady?'

'No, I'm afraid I don't smoke,' I apologised.

She looked at me with disdain, then pulling herself up into a sergeant-majorish stance, shouted across the ward:

' 'Ere Audrey, you've got a visitor!'

Somewhere amid the crowd a voice replied:

'Oo is it?'

My little hostess looked at me.

'Wot's your name?'

I decided to bring some influence to bear on her and said, 'The Reverend Frank Wilson.'

'It's a Reverend!' she cried out and from the huddle came the reply from the same voice:

'I don't know no reverends!'

They all giggled and every eye was turned on me. Jane, my presenter, for that was her name, backed away reverently and for a moment I was alone, then:

'Oh blimey, it's 'im!' and Audrey appeared. 'You came, like you said you would.' She shuffled over to where I stood.

'Yes,' I said, smiling and holding out my hand, 'I'm sorry I didn't get here sooner.' She grasped my hand with a podgy nicotine stained one of her own and without looking into my face motioned to a part of the room which seemed relatively private.

I studied this girl; she was in her twenties, she said, but years of drug abuse had aged her tragically. Her black hair was cropped short, her jeans were baggy and torn. Her eyes, when she allowed me to see her face, were sad and empty.

She told me about herself. She was an orphan, unwanted and unloved. She had come to London three or four years previously, attracted by the lure of easy money and bright lights. She'd been in the WRAF for a brief time until, as she put it, 'They chucked me out!' She'd been inside a woman's prison and involved herself in all sorts of sordid things, including arranging sex orgies with other young hippy boys and girls in the West End of London for rich tourists who were prepared to pay for such depravity.

She was soon using drugs – smoking at first. A little pot, a few pills and then heroin. Twice she had almost died and the skill of an emergency team had saved her life.

'Not that I can see the point of it, my life's pretty useless,' she said.

Her present time in the locked ward of the hospital was due to her involvement with criminal activities and she had 'got caught'.

'There's no hope here,' she kept saying. 'I'll soon be chucked out without a cure. I don't even seem to be able to live without drugs.'

She suddenly turned and looked intently up at me: 'When I was in the children's home, they used to tell us about God, but I never bothered with it – you said in your letter there was hope for me, do you think God would bother with me, no one else ever has?'

'When you discover the reality of Jesus Christ, Audrey,' I said '. . . you find a new dimension in living. He helps you not only to live without drugs, but he gives purpose to life so that we no longer merely exist, but really discover what life is for!'

'And what is it for?' she was interested.

'Well, above all, man's main reason for living is to dis- cover and glorify God. I can think of nothing more terrible than to live a life of no purpose at all and to suddenly arrive at old age with nothing having been achieved and unready to face death and God!'

'Well I've achieved rock bottom, I'm a junky and a useless one at that,' Audrey said. 'I guess the addict lives the most pointless life of all.'

'Well,' I replied, 'many respectable and successful people from a material point of view, are no more ready for death and God than the young beat up junky! All of us can get right with God if we really want to.'

'I really want to.' Audrey's lifeless eyes filled with tears. 'Really I do!' and she sobbed.

I paid many calls on Audrey in the following weeks and visited many of her friends on the ward whom she introduced to me. Shirley suggested that when she was allowed to make visits out, that as she had no one to go to, she could come to our little house. This she did, although often she only got as far as Soho where some addict or pusher would sell her drugs and she'd be taken back to the hospital by the police or social workers. However, we stuck with her and as time went on she opened up more and more to the God whom she felt was so remote to her. What's more, he opened to her and often she would share with us how even though she kept running, he was never very far away.

How we came to love this young girl who gradually was regaining some of her cheerfulness and humour. Then one Saturday in early 1967 she found Christ. It was at our first annual meeting in the Metropolitan Tabernacle. Eric Hutchings had been our guest preacher and he had given such a powerful message and invited people to come forward to accept Christ. Audrey was among them and I drew her aside as she smilingly and tearfully walked down the church.

'Audrey, what are you doing?'

'I can't keep " 'im" out of my life any more. I want God,' she said, 'now.'

That evening Audrey Williams met Jesus Christ. Warmth and love and acceptance flowed into her. She wasn't alone any longer. The search was over, although the battle was not yet won over drugs.

I continued visiting Dr Chapple's clinic for addicts, and learned a great deal under his instruction. When he asked me to be the chaplain for his own proposed treatment centre I knew that this highly knowledgeable medical man was recognising a deep need in his patients which could only be met by a spiritual answer.

In the midst of all these comings and goings there was an important arrival – that of our third daughter. Now we had Christina, Stephanie and baby Kathy. By this time a seasoned 'expectant father', I was thrilled to assist the midwife in the birth, doing all the traditional things like carrying around steaming kettles and towels and making the tea!

Shirley wasn't well for quite a long time after Kathy's arrival, and it was quite a blow when we realised that the return of the Claxtons was not far off and we must again turn our attention to the recurring problem of somewhere to live. Dr Claxton's lovely home had been a haven, but the time had come to move. As it turned out our next home was very different.

Wheels were set in motion when I had a phone call one day from an evangelist called Roger Forster. He was then leading a Bible teaching ministry among a group of young Christians living as a community in a large house in Erith, Kent. The group were moving out soon. Would Life for the World like to buy it to start their work among addicts?

This really made me laugh a little, knowing that the newly formed Life for the World council didn't have two pennies to rub together! Obviously the word had got around about the forming of a council and the assumption was made that such an organisation must be backed by capital.

However, Roger Forster came to see me, and I explained to him that buying his house was out of the question. But the outcome of our conversation was that Roger offered me two attic rooms in the house for us to stay in while we looked round for accommodation. So, just a few weeks later, we moved into two rather dingy attic rooms, praying that it wouldn't be long before we could be a little more settled.

Trying to do what was right was often a real struggle with my conscience as I thought of all the difficulties I involved my family in, but whereas there were plenty of words of recrimination and criticism from others, there were none from Shirley. She believed wholeheartedly in what I was doing.

Several young addicts I knew died during this period. One was an eighteen-year-old boy I met in hospital, contacted through a Christian Probation Officer. I only saw Steve once. He was being put through a programme of medical withdrawal but died quite suddenly. The doctors diagnosed a malignant cancer. They were not sure if the cancer had been caused by drugs.

But the days were not all dark. For the hundreds we saw turn away and get lost in degradation and some in death there were the handful who responded – and they were really worth everything! The name Life for the World ceased to sound unfamiliar to us, and many others were coming to hear of it for the first time and becoming interested in the work. It was a special encouragement to me when the minister of the large Kensington Temple church in London, the Rev. Eldin Corsie, pledged his support to the work. He readily accepted an invitation to become a Council member. We proudly transferred our meetings to the vestry of the church. Life for the World had a London venue!

Meanwhile we were involved in giving some really practical help to the young married couple we had met, John and Jackie Blake. As we had hoped and expected, the Baptist church in St Leonards, led by Gordon Hunt, were willing to do all they could to help them. John had been given a job by an Italian couple who were church members. They ran a restaurant on the sea front and John became a waiter there. The women of the church had found the couple a basement flat in the town. It was bare and scruffy but they did their best to make it more homely and the result was certainly an improvement. Shirley had suggested that we give them some of our own furniture that we had put in store and so a number of our bits and pieces were added to really cheer the place up.

So John and Jackie had a home – but perhaps more importantly they became a family again. We contacted the local authorities involved and after a lot of red tape they agreed to give back the children as long as there was a proper home and John was able to provide for them.

It was with very mixed feelings that we drove John and Jackie to the foster parents' home to pick up the children. The foster mother looked tearful and obviously sceptical. The two children shuffled their feet and hunched their shoulders into duffle coats several sizes too big. They were suspicious of the Mum and Dad they knew but vaguely. Could John and Jackie wipe away their bad dreams with a new start and a lot of love and responsibility?

We decided to abandon our anxieties. Surely they would be safe in a little out-of-the-way place like St Leonards! John and Jackie were attending a clinic and following a gradually reducing course of substitute drugs. They had been responsive when Gordon and I talked to them about Christian things and had promised to attend the church. We prayed with them as we left them to start their new life together. Their future was full of promise and we longed for it all to be fully realised.

Meanwhile, the need for my own family accommodation

apart, Life for the World was trying to make a dream into a reality. Our conviction continued to be that the greatest benefit we could give to young addicts was a home far from the availability of drugs, where they could take an honest look at themselves and the reasons why they had turned to drugs. We longed for a home that spoke more than a hundred sermons – a home where a lost young person could experience life and love in a Christian family atmosphere and find for himself strength to overcome his drug problem through a personal faith in Jesus Christ.

How excited Shirley and I were one day to be setting off to see the first house – a large ruined farmhouse in East Anglia. We made the drive in a borrowed car, the one that had been given to us having expired some time before. Someone else bought the farmhouse – at the asking price of £3,000. We weren't dismayed. 'The Lord has something better for us!' said Council member Don Lewis. It didn't matter that this wasn't the one for us. We had started our house-hunting for God.

Our next excursion was to a stately home in Scotland! This was an enormous beautifully maintained house in Jedburgh, formerly the home of a Scottish peer. The administrators of the estate were very sympathetic to us but the idea of drug addicts filling the house really daunted them – not forgetting of course that we still had nothing like the colossal sum needed for the house!

We looked at many houses over the next few months. Then one day we went to Epsom to see an old mansion which was in a dilapidated state but was protected by a preservation order. The property development company who owned it had advertised asking for suggestions! When we arrived we drew up alongside an immaculate Rolls-Royce. Inside was a very glum looking agent. He'd arrived a little earlier to find that lead thieves had completely stripped the roof and torrential rain had flooded through the house. The lovely ballroom was ankle deep in dirty water and plasterwork was crumbling.

Well, that was another potential home for Life for the World that we crossed off the list! However, news of something a little more modest in the way of accommodation was waiting for us on our return home. Roger Forster had called to see us and left a note. A friend of his who was a missionary in Africa owned a house in Harrow and was looking for a Christian couple to take it over while he was abroad. Roger had decided that it was just the thing for us.

Shirley and I left almost immediately to have a look at it. It was an ordinary three bedroomed semi-detached furnished house in Tintern Way. We looked over it and decided that this should be the next step from our two little attic rooms. We sat on the stairs together. Pockets and handbag were unceremoniously emptied and we added what we found to the small sum we knew was in our bank balance. We just had the twenty pounds necessary to secure the house and pay the first month's rent in advance.

A few hectic days later we made the move into this house with our three little girls and Susie – a fluffy tabby kitten that Shirley had somehow acquired. While Shirley began to unpack cardboard boxes of belongings I went out to find the local shops for a few groceries. On my way back I had to pass road works on the corner of Tintern Way. As I stepped my way over the rubble that had spilled on to the pavement a voice broke into my faraway thoughts. It was the voice of God, speaking to me and as he had done on the railway station; as he had done so many times before to encourage and lead me. 'As surely as you have turned this corner in the road so I have caused you to turn

5

a corner in your life, and you will never go this way again.'
I held my breath and my heart overflowed with love for
this wonderful God. God had promised another new
chapter – and I couldn't wait to get to the opening
paragraph!

6

1966 was a wonderful year for Life for the World. It was a year of building up, of real growth, of recognition and results.

In particular, three men had independently seen the vision of the work I was doing. They were my own pastor, Pastor Rudman, John Sadler, the man who had first introduced me to the Lord Jesus, and Don Lewis, treasurer of the Sussex Crusade led by Dr Eric Hutchings.

One other supporter assumed a very important role during this time at Harrow; Jack Jenner. Jack was a quiet but brilliant agricultural graduate I had first met when I was minister of the church in Kent. A fuzzy-edged picture often in my mind showed Jack bending over a field of young plants, working a farm next to the house, the house which God was to give us for young people. A romantic dream? An overworked imagination? Or a glimpse of promises fulfilled?

Jack moved into our third bedroom at Tintern Way. Visiting prisons, hospitals, seeking out addicts in the late-night London underworld – Jack began to share in the work in every way. He was a good singer and musician and dedicated these talents to God and to the little public meetings Life for the World held to inform and challenge ordinary men and women.

But it wasn't just the ordinary men and women who were willing to listen. Men in higher positions, holding important posts in Government, the legal profession, the social services and medicine – many wanted to know about our work, and I began to find myself involved in interviews with the prominent and wealthy which set my heart thumping and my knees knocking. Walking the streets of the big city had not seemed to make me any less a stumbling country boy, unversed in diplomacy, far from professional.

One morning I sat trembling in the outer office of a big suite of plush executive offices off Oxford Circus. I had been granted an interview with Sir Alfred Owen.

As the minutes ticked by the secretary repeatedly apologised for Sir Alfred's lateness and this only served to deepen my general foot-shuffling embarrassment. What was I doing here taking up the valuable time of this important man? How could I coherently express to him the heart of the work of Life for the World and gain his interest and support?

Finally the door opened and in swept a man whose very ordinary appearance took me by surprise. Having never met a 'Sir' before my anxiety had manufactured an ogre in top hat and ermine tails who grew more grotesque with each tick-tock of the clock.

Sir Alfred smiled. 'Mr Wilson? So sorry I'm late. Do come in.'

Words tumbled out of me with the speed of a runaway

train. Sir Alfred listened impassively, and let me talk for my allotted time.

'Yes, well, Mr Wilson, if I was to give everyone who came to me with schemes for opening houses for this or that worthy cause my financial backing I'd soon be a poor man. But keep me informed. Good-bye.'

A brisk handshake. Suddenly I was outside, my thoughts drowned by the Oxford Circus traffic chaos. And Sir Alfred was off to his next appointment. I felt foolish. So much for my opportunity to interest a man of influence. A waste of time? It proved not to be. A week later a letter arrived from Sir Alfred, enclosing a cheque for one hundred pounds! It was an unbelievably large gift to us in those days. But, more important than the gift, that nerve-wracking interview was the start of a warm friendship which continued for many years.

Meanwhile, in quiet St Leonards-on-Sea, all was far from well!

'Can you come straight away, Frank?' It was Gordon Hunt's worried voice on the telephone.

We had thought John and Jackie and the two children safe in this quiet out-of-the-way place. However, we had reckoned without their 'friends' who had picked up news that the couple had a new 'pad' in Sussex and decided to pay a visit. Jackie responded immediately to the offer of drugs from these faces from the past who turned up on the doorstep, and John's resistance had melted within a week. It was only a matter of weeks before the couple were well and truly hooked again on heroin and cocaine, with a ready access to as much as they could buy.

As I drove down to Sussex I knew I couldn't make any recriminations against Gordon and his church members. They had done all they could within the scope of their limited knowledge of all the facets of the problem. They had cared. They had given. But it hadn't been enough. My heart was heavy. If only there was somewhere we could take them, and watch over them like we did our own children, protect them from the past intruding its ugly face on the present until they were strong enough to face the future.

I drove straight to the little flat. Shouting and banging noises reached me before I got to the door bell. I was let in by one of the women members of the church, who disappeared into the bedroom. I caught sight of two pale-faced children sitting lifelessly on the unmade bed.

John was nowhere to be seen but in the living-room Gordon was trying to restrain and reason with an hysterical Jackie.

'Frank,' she screamed, 'Frank, it's not fair. Make him give me back my drugs.'

The little flat that willing hands had made so clean and cheerful just a few months before was dark, damp and utterly depressing. A makeshift curtain obliterated almost all daylight, the little dining table I recognised as the one Shirley and I had given was stained and littered with unwashed crockery and the sordid evidence of injecting drugs. Everything was dirty, a mirror cracked, a chair broken and propped against a child's rusty tricycle.

Hope had gone out of the room, and decay and degradation taken its place. Jackie was a wild jerky figure in dirty jeans and a shrunken faded sweater trying to snatch a bottle of pills Gordon was holding behind his back.

Our joint efforts to persuade Jackie to forget her drugs, sit down and talk things out with us turned into a violent physical battle. Her rage gave her uncontrollable strength. At one stage she grabbed a razor from a drawer, alternately threatening to attack us if we came near or to slash her own wrists if we didn't return her pills.

It was a hateful scene. With a sudden rush we managed between us to pin her on the floor and prise the razor blade from her fingers. And it was at this moment that John arrived.

Jackie calmed down when she saw John. But still we had to give in, returning her pills which she immediately prepared and injected with desperate haste. The couple made it clear that they had decided to go their own way; they didn't want our help any more. I felt overwhelmingly sad. Sad for John and Jackie. Sad for the little children that I'd helped to have returned to them. Sad for Gordon and his helpers from the church. All we could do now was to keep our distance but keep in touch, be close enough to be available if they needed us.

John and Jackie were rejecting God's way, but other addicts were responding. When I first met Jackie she had told me of a 'vision' of Jesus she claimed to have had. I remained sceptical. Many addicts I met invented 'spiritual phenomena' or feigned fervent religious zeal to ingratiate themselves with me to get a free meal, and I gradually learned not to be taken in by them.

However, one young addict had a dramatic religious experience which I could not doubt.

'I don't understand what it all means. But yesterday when I was arrested I was nobody, a drug addict with no concern for anyone but me and anything but my next fix. But last night in the prison cell I met God. Yes, God! I woke up in the middle of the night and God was there. I was an atheist yesterday, but today I believe.'

Tim repeated to me the same incredible story that he had told the court. The shocked magistrates didn't know what to do, but a young Methodist minister, David Copestake, had been in court and he had referred Tim to me to see if I could help.

Uninhibited tears rolled down Tim's face as we talked, sitting on the narrow wooden bench outside the court-room. Tim wanted to know God in his life. I couldn't doubt his sincerity and made a rapid decision. This broken young man was to be the first Life for the World resident. Would Tim come home with me? Anything, he said, as long as he could find out about faith in God.

Half-an-hour later I made my first court appearance, as nervously as if I was on trial myself. In a strange way I was. I described Life for the World and its aims to the bench of solemn magistrates, and asked if I could take Tim into my home and my care.

Tim was given a conditional discharge for the drugs offences and our home became his for the next three months. The first few weeks were very difficult as he en-countered the very real physical and emotional pains of withdrawal from drugs. But Tim himself handed over his bag of drugs and syringes the day he moved in, for me to destroy, and his own determination was a tremendous advantage.

Tim was one of the many intensely individual young people I met who, out of folly or misplaced search for adventure or purpose, had wandered into the suffocating trap of drug abuse. Yes, there were many of those who epitomised the typical sketch of the addict – long-haired, foul-mouthed, unwashed, hardened criminals. But others, like Tim, could not be glibly classified by any common factor except addiction itself. Some I met were well-groomed, some were gifted, some were academically brilliant.

7

Chris was very much an individual, too, as I discovered during the period of many months in which I followed him around from dingy bedsitter to dingy bedsitter.

My first visit to Chris was made after I had met Mary, a tearful young art student who had been living with him in Richmond. Mary was infatuated with Chris, but hated his addiction, and lived in fear of either Chris being arrested or herself becoming pregnant. Heartbroken, she said she had decided to leave Chris. Could I help him?

I stood outside an imposing four-storey house in Richmond some days later, feeling very nervous, as I usually did when setting out to introduce myself to an addict for the first time.

I went up a flight of six wide stone steps, through the open doors and into a large bare hallway. My footsteps echoed on the tiled floor, and immediately a dishevelled woman in a headscarf and grubby apron appeared as if from nowhere.

'Yea? Whaddyou want?'

A cigarette dangled from her open mouth, and a bucket full of dirty water from one hand.

I asked for Chris, describing him as well as I could, realising that I didn't even know his surname.

The woman looked doubtful.

'A young man . . . er . . . there was a young lady living with him until . . .'

She laughed coarsely.

'My dear,' she spluttered, 'they're all like that 'ere. The 'ole 'ouse is full of 'em, all livin' together. I 'spect you mean that rum 'un downstairs, in the basement. Try there.'

She disappeared through a dark doorway as suddenly as she had appeared, the clanking of her metal pail echoing after her.

There was a telephone coinbox in the hall. I went over and lifted the receiver to ring Shirley. No dialling tone. The coinbox had been broken into.

Feeling even more nervous, I went back down the stone steps, and then I spotted a flight of smaller steps leading down below street level. At the bottom I squeezed past a window to reach the door, and as I did so I heard a scuffling noise and saw shadowy movements.

Well, I'd been seen, so there was no going back. I knocked. And knocked again. I waited in the ominous silence. I knocked again, then turned to go when I heard the sound of a key grating in a lock.

The door creaked open about six inches. Just enough to release a strong odour of old tramps. Another two inches and in the gloom I could make out two staring bloodshot eyes.

'What do you want?' The voice was hoarse. But also frightened. I began to relax.

'Mary asked me to come and . . .'

He swore, flung open the door and roughly pulled me inside, banging the door shut behind me.

I stood blinking in the darkened room. It was three o'clock in the afternoon, but no ray of sunshine penetrated this little airless room, and Chris had obviously just got up.

He was quite a character, I thought, taking in his long flowing brown hair, long bushy beard, faded pyjama bottoms and shrunken black jumper.

'Cor, you look like the flippin' fuzz!'

I apologised. It wasn't something I'd thought of, but I suppose I might have looked a bit daunting, even official. Today was cold and my large frame was amply covered in a big black overcoat!

'Hang on, mate.' He dived under the bed and produced a syringe. I realised that he must have been in the middle of fixing when I knocked.

He gestured to me to sit down while he was making a tourniquet round his upper arm. Without hesitation he plunged the needle into the raised, bloody vein in his arm and began to 'flush' – pulling the syringe up and down, mixing his own blood with the last traces of his precious drugs.

Suddenly everything blurred and I realised with horror that if I didn't take a firm grip on myself I was going to faint. It was the same sensation I remembered when, as a very young minister, I had been called into a front room to witness a body laid out for a funeral for the first time. Respectful relatives had hovered round me with comments like 'Aye, Mr Wilson, don't he look grand, never saw him looking so peaceful. Sleepin' like a babe, he is!'

I gripped the edge of my chair and took gulps of the stale air. Chris finished fixing, but was so obviously 'high' that I knew it was useless trying to get through to him. I told him who I was, but he began to ramble incoherent sentences and I left, telling him I'd be back.

This first rather abortive visit was followed by many more, increasingly less difficult as Chris came to trust me and began to talk freely. But the visits were particularly memorable because of a big mistake I made! On my second visit to Chris he made me promise not to mention 'religion'. I agreed, thinking rather naïvely that if I could establish a friendly relationship perhaps Chris would ask questions about my faith. I soon regretted my promise.

The best time to visit Chris, I discovered, was about midday, just as he was eating breakfast – doughnuts, biscuits, and very sweet tea made with condensed milk. As we got to know each other better I felt very frustrated about my rash promise not to talk about 'religion', for here was a young man who really needed to have his life revolutionised.

One day when I arrived, Mary was there. She didn't give an explanation. She didn't need to – she had already told me about her feelings for Chris and she hadn't been able to stay away any longer. That afternoon, with Chris's permission, a young student friend was going to help me make an 8mm film of Chris fixing his drugs, which we were going to use as part of some publicity for Life for the World.

We set up the equipment, and Chris went into his usual routine, not at all inhibited by the camera which I was aiming at him. David, my young friend, was holding the lights.

Suddenly it went dark.

'Don't be silly, David! Put the lights back on!'

There was no answer. David, ashen faced, was lying in an unconscious heap on the floor!

Chris, like several others, seemed to feel a personal

responsibility to educate me in the life of the addict and often took me to places in the West End to meet and talk with other addicts he knew.

Having set myself the problem of not being able to talk to Chris directly about the things of God, I developed the habit of silently praying for him whenever he was injecting.

One afternoon, sitting in another gloomy bedsitter littered with the junkie's equipment, I was praying with a note of desperation. 'Lord, forgive me for my promise. Now I'm not free to tell Chris about you. Please get through to him, even though I can't. Come into this room and speak to him yourself.'

I became aware that I was being watched, and opened my eyes. Chris had stopped fixing and was glaring at me.

'I thought I told you not to mention . . . him.'

'Who?'

'God,' he said accusingly.

'I didn't say a word.'

He looked embarrassed. 'Well, it's gone all . . . all religious in here, so cut it out!'

Poor Chris! He felt tricked – but I felt triumphant! Chris had turned his back on God, but God was here all the same.

A crisis point finally came when Mary left Chris again, this time for good. She was leaving college and returning to her parents' home. Chris was shattered. He'd slept around with many girls, but Mary, he said, was 'different'.

'She was a cut above the rest, Frank, wasn't she?'

He buried his shaggy face in his hands. I knew he wouldn't turn away from the name of Jesus now and I began to talk to him about the need in his life to change in the dramatic definite way that only turning to Christ could bring. His hostility was gone.

'All right. I do need help, and I am ready to listen. But I can't stay here, Frank.'

What could I do? Our little house was already bursting at the seams with our three little girls, Jack, and the many unannounced visitors who often bedded down on the floor in the front room.

I thought of one of the Life for the World Council members, John Noble, who'd often offered help. I looked at the crumpled young man beside me and decided I couldn't waste a minute. I went out to find the nearest phone box.

John and his wife Christine said at once that they would take him in. They were a warm-hearted young couple with three small children, and within a couple of hours they were welcoming one rather reticent and bedraggled young addict into their home.

I prayed that it would work out. Chris was one of society's rejects, an 'undesirable'. Could a loving Christian family change him?

Murray, in contrast, was far from being an 'undesirable'. In fact, though an addict, Murray was the perfect gentleman. He never appeared on our Harrow doorstep without a bouquet of roses which he would ceremoniously present to Shirley.

My first encounter with Murray was in Dr Chapple's new drug treatment clinic in Chelsea. Dr Chapple had left the hospital set-up to pioneer his clinic, then a totally new concept in the treatment of addiction.

'If anyone needs religion it's Murray,' said Dr Chapple. and that was my cue to take a special interest in this well-educated twenty-year-old.

Murray was a great talker. He talked of the gentle things of life which he obviously appreciated so much and with which he tried to surround his life. He described to me his loving mother, his beautiful actress sister, afternoon teas on the lawn at home during the heat of the summer, his own neat, tastefully decorated flat. He expanded on the merits of good food and his favourite expensive brand of coffee.

But in spite of the seeming perfection of his neatly ordered life, Murray was heavily addicted to heroin. The drug had already begun to age his body and doctors gave him just two or three more years of life unless he gave up drugs.

One day when I was talking to Murray in the clinic, the conversation didn't take the usual extravagant lines. Without any prompting Murray wanted to talk quite seriously on the subject of life and death. He seemed unusually clear in his thinking.

'I wish I could know God.' The remark was sudden, wistful.

'You know, Frank. Really know God. Like you do.' The words came out with an obvious struggle.

He meant it! Our conversation developed and extended well into the evening. We hardly noticed the passing of the hours. Murray was so engrossed in what I had to say and I felt so thrilled at having this unhindered opportunity to talk to an open heart and an open mind about Jesus.

Lights began to flicker off in the corridors. The clinic was closing for the day.

A few streets away Murray let us into his tiny flat. Many bright, gay paintings hung on the walls, some by Murray himself.

We continued our earnest conversation over mugs of coffee. I sat on his divan bed, and Murray on the carpeted floor, leaning back against the wall.

It was about four o'clock in the morning when Murray lifted himself up on to his knees and began praying, pouring out his need to know Jesus as his Saviour. It was a cry from an empty heart and I knew that God heard and answered instantly. Murray began to cry, then to shout 'It works! It works!' He hugged me, his face shining, stumbling over words in a clumsy effort to describe a totally new experience – an awareness of the presence of God, a warmth, a deep happiness.

Those rewarding dawn hours were the prelude to Murray's many visits to our home, always bringing armfuls of roses for Shirley, with whom he struck up a very good and close relationship. He continued to attend Dr Chapple's clinic daily, following a course of gradually reducing maintenance drugs. He hated this, he longed to be free of his addiction completely but his physical dependence was such that he did not have the strength to dispense at once with the habit he now despised.

I felt very keenly that here was a very vulnerable young man, newly born into the family of God. The hard veneer of the addict culture was gradually stripped away. Murray was a new person now that he had given his heart and life to Jesus. I had taken the initiative. I had introduced him to his new life. In a very real sense he was my responsibility. Murray and the handful of others who responded positively to the Gospel were all my burden. I carried them around with me every day. It was a very wonderful privilege, yet a frightening responsibility. I knew that their vulnerability was such that at any moment they might be snatched back into their old world. I felt painfully inadequate to protect them during the time necessary for them to build up their own defences.

Lord, please, what about my house? My refuge? These

young people, Lord Jesus, they need a sanctuary, a house in the country, a house of new beginnings.

Then we heard of a house for sale in Faringdon, Wiltshire, that made us all feel quite excited. The only Life for the World Council member with a reasonable car was Don Lewis, who had an old Jaguar, so one day five of us plus Don squeezed into it in high spirits. There was Don, myself, Jack Jenner, Gordon Hunt from St Leonard's-on-Sea, Eldin Corsie from Kensington Temple and a Mr Jardine, a friend of Rev Hand of Swindon, who wanted to support the work financially.

The house was a great rambling old mansion in very good condition with several acres of farmland, and we were suitably impressed as we were shown over it by a polite agent.

Of course, this was not the first such house we had inspected, but each time our hopes rose inexplicably. House hunting for God was an exciting business. We must often have given the air of being an improbable group of eccentric, perhaps slightly disreputable millionaires as we examined these various properties. On leaving we would use the same rather pompous phrase: 'We have one more partner who has to be consulted. If he's in agreement there'll be no problem about the money.' We would all nod mysteriously and none of the agents as they courteously showed us out guessed that the anonymous partner was God himself!

The house in Faringdon looked suitable. Mr Jardine promised to give £2,000 if we could raise the balance – £23,000! at that time the total annual income of the Trust was about £400. We prayed about this house but the partner holding the purse strings remained silent and a few weeks later the sale went through – to someone else.

Undeterred, we resumed the search. And this time our

6

attention focused on a lovely old house on the southern edge of the Cotswolds, some miles from Bristol. Fellfield House, which was owned by an Australian peer, was offered for sale at £14,000. We sent out a picture of the house with an appeal letter to our faithful prayer partners and raised £1,500. The bank were willing to loan £8,000. But as the weeks passed the gap between the Life for the World bank balance and the magical sum of £14,000 didn't narrow.

Finally the agent rang to say that they had received a better offer for Fellfield. We had one week to raise the necessary money. The next seven days passed uneventfully and we resigned ourselves to abandoning the house, returning the bank loan, and starting again.

Reviewing our completely barren efforts to get a home for a need which every day seemed to increase in urgency, I felt crushed and frustrated. What was wrong? At every step we seemed to come up against a brick wall. I examined my own heart. No, my conviction that this was God's will, that this was the work he had called me to, had in no way lessened, in spite of terrific pressures to give up the whole project. Depression and a sense of failure swallowed me up and I no longer felt able to resist.

8

'Brother!' boomed the voice of Don Lewis, 'I have found the house of the Lord's choice.'

It was a few days after the loss of Fellfield and as I answered the telephone in an irritated frame of mind I could only resent Don's enthusiastic tones.

'Really? What? Another one!'

I regretted the bitter reply as soon as I had spoken it, but Don was unabashed.

'This really is it. Oh, you'll love it! It's enormous!'

'How enormous?' I was now making an effort to be polite.

'Oh, hundreds of rooms. Hundreds! It's got everything. Magnificent rooms, lovely grounds, an ornamental lake, tennis courts. Needs a bit of doing to it, but, well, we'll manage,' he said cheerfully.

'Well, where exactly is this marvellous place?'

Don explained that it was outside a small Gloucestershire village. He had been visiting his daughter, who lived in a cottage at the side of what turned out to be the driveway of an empty mansion.

'There's just something about this place. Now, Frank, you must ring straight away. The agents are Alfred Savill and Sons.'

I jotted down the same, promised Don I would ring and said good-bye. I sat staring at the name on the telephone pad for several minutes. Another wild goose chase? I was tired of searching for a dream. My heart was weary with disappointment.

Still, God knew. And if it was God's work what right had I to give up? Something of Don's enthusiasm began to stir in me. His excited words tripped round inside my head. 'You'll love it . . . the house of the Lord's choice.'

Even as I dialled my depression was lifting.

I didn't even know the name of the property, but the friendly female voice was very helpful.

'Oh, yes, sir, that would be Northwick Park Mansion, just outside Blockley village, near Moreton-in-Marsh. That's Mr Thistlethwayte's department. He's one of the senior partners of the firm. Please hold the line and I'll see if he's available.'

Mr Thistlethwayte was available. There was a rustling of papers as he began to read out with polite precision a description of Northwick Park Mansion.

The details bombarded me. Over sixty rooms . . . three hundred-year-old stately home . . . art gallery . . . orangery . . . stables and outbuildings . . . pleasure gardens . . . servants' quarters . . .

'A magnificent property in its time, Mr Wilson. But unfortunately the last owner was something of an eccentric and sadly the house has been seriously neglected for many years, years which have taken a heavy toll on the complete structure of the house.

'All in all, a prospective buyer would need to be a person of very substantial means.'

I took a deep breath. 'How substantial?' I heard myself asking.

'Oh, around £200,000.'

£200,000! Had we taken leave of our senses! Everyone could quite rightly accuse us of suffering from delusions of grandeur! £200,000! Why, the Lord couldn't raise £14,000 for Fellfield – why should we even consider a house of such an astronomical sum!

'Are you still there, Mr Wilson?'

Another deep breath. It was an effort to sound calm.

'Would you consider, I mean, would it be at all possible to ... to rent it?'

'Well, the owners might consider it, but even so you must realise that it would still entail a considerable sum. Then of course there would be the substantial sum necessary to render the house fit for occupation.'

The recurrent word 'substantial' hung in the air like a heavy black cloud. Just as heavy as the large manilla envelope which arrived for me in the post the following morning, promptly following my request to Mr Thistlethwayte to 'let me have all the details'.

I thumbed through pages of plans, measurements and descriptions. It all added up to a wonderful seventeenth-century mansion, designed for all the elaborate grandeur of a bygone era.

The description of the house enchanted me. But it was more than sentimentality or appreciation of the architecture. I had a growing conviction that this really could be the house of the Lord's choice. For some reason that could only be attributed to the Spirit of God within me, I knew that this house really was different. Could God bring it to pass, that Life for the World should have this wonderful house? As I thought about the apparent impossibility of such a thing, I felt a strange curiosity and excitement to see just how God would work it all out!

The huge size, the dreadful deterioration of the property – no, they didn't seem problems at all. I laid my hands on the plans and whispered 'Lord, give us this house.'

I decided to present Mr Thistlethwayte with the truth, and rang him immediately. I told him about Life for the World, our aims in finding a home for addicts, and admitted that the Trust was virtually penniless. To my utter amazement he was very sympathetic to my rather extraordinary confession, and as I put down the phone I could only stare stupidly at the scribbled note on my desk diary.

'Next Friday. 11 a.m. Meet bailiff. Northwick Park.'

The next few days were strangely exhilarating. The thought of Friday's appointment was with me as I continued my hectic daily round of visits to addicts, in homes, hospitals and prisons, and the nightly excursions to 'heartbreak corner'.

But suddenly there was an added dimension to all I was seeking to do. I seemed to have so much more to offer. The dream of having a house in the country was now a very real possibility. Northwick Park wasn't just another house.

'Hello, Frank. Christine Noble here. Can you come over? We seem to have reached some kind of turning point with Chris, and we need your help.'

I left for the Noble's home, wondering what was happening to my shaggy bearded friend.

'He's shut himself in his room and won't come out.'

I sat on the settee in the comfortable living-room while Christine told me briefly about Chris's stay with them over the past months. John and Christine had insisted on Chris joining them in reading from the Bible each morning at the breakfast table. Chris agreed, but each chapter only seemed to give him fuel for never-ending arguments which he battled out with Christine round the house for the rest of the day. It became almost a game. Each day Chris would present her with a new and carefully thought out argument against a certain point of Christian doctrine. What does the Bible say about this? And that? Back would come ready answers from Christine and Chris would retire with a frown to think again.

'This morning,' said Christine, 'he really thought he'd won.'

He had bounced down the stairs into the kitchen.

'I've got it. Here's something the Bible doesn't know about. So much for God having all the answers! Now, if you can prove to me that this Jesus guy knew what it was like to be like me – to be an addict – then, then I'll believe!'

Christine emptied the washing up bowl, dried her hands and opened up her Bible. She began to read about how Jesus was 'tempted in all points' as an ordinary man, yet 'without sin'. And then the description of the suffering Christ by Isaiah: 'He is despised and rejected of men; a man of sorrows and acquainted with grief . . . he was despised . . . wounded . . . bruised for our iniquities. The Lord hath laid on him the iniquity of us all.'

'You see, Chris, my Saviour hung on the cross for the sins of the whole world, meaning he personally bore the sin and sorrow of every single individual. He took on himself all the pain and degradation of every individual, all the agony of the junkie, every needle mark he felt. God hid his face when his beloved Son was crushed under the rottenness of me, of you.'

'What happened next, Christine?'

'Frank, I thought he was going to explode with rage. He ran from the room, rushed upstairs and slammed the door.'

Filled with apprehension I mounted the stairs and tapped gently on the door of Chris's room.

'Come in.' His voice was low and emotional.

'She's got me, Frank. That woman's really got me. I can't run any more, I can't argue.'

'What do you mean?'

'Well, now I really know. I really know. I can't argue against God any more. I've got to believe.'

9

It was a golden July day. A faint morning mist was lifting lazily over the fields. Don Lewis and I exchanged excited grins as we sped through the leafy lanes.

The Gloucestershire countryside was beautiful, green and refreshing. We turned out of Moreton-in-Marsh on to the road to Blockley. A few miles along the road a sign-post directed us off to the right and we entered a narrow winding road flanked with pasture, gently leading down into a little valley which sheltered the village. The hill gradually steepened and suddenly we were entering Blockley.

Yellow Cotswold stone houses and cottages clustered and leaned together along the narrow main street. A pretty village with all the traditional assets – an old village church, bowling green, several small shops, an old bridge over a stream.

Out of the village and a mile up the road past rows of neat allotments, we came to an entrance. There was the cottage where Don's daughter lived. We drove past, and then through an old stone gateway on a bend in a long driveway.

Twenty or thirty yards further on the trees thinned, giving me my first glimpse of a magnificent imposing house built of the same lovely warm mellow Cotswold stone. Northwick Park Mansion. My heart jumped for joy. It was all I had imagined. No – it was much more!

At the top of the driveway a man was waiting by a low stone wall. He advanced to meet us, hand outstretched. It was the bailiff, Mr Warner, a man in his late fifties, tall, well-built, with a kind, warm country face.

Guided by him we picked our way through shoulder-high weeds and nettles past a derelict stable block and then across a cobbled courtyard to a back entrance. Mr Warner produced an enormous heavy key which gratingly turned in the lock.

The door swung back on rusty hinges. My first view of the house had been that of a warm and golden castle in the air, but the opening door revealed the dreadful decay of the interior. Brown painted walls were damp, cracked and peeling, windows were barred and shuttered, the bare flagstones littered with crumbling fragments of stone and wood and a thick layer of dust.

We stepped inside and heard the scurrying of rats. I shivered. We were in part of the servants' quarters, perhaps a kitchen. We walked along narrow corridors with uneven floors and low beams, peering into tiny bare rooms. A twisting flight of wooden steps led to more little rooms, all gloomily shuttered, and then to a long room with great metal hooks for hanging salted meat carcasses suspended from the beams. In some places a little light filtered in through holes in the roof, showing up rotten floor boards where rain had continually poured through.

Then we passed from this L-shaped wing into the

grander side of the house. We stood at the bottom of a marvellous central circular staircase, running up from a reception hall through three storeys, with doors all the way up leading into huge high-ceilinged guest rooms. At the top of the staircase was a domed roof made of coloured glass. A trio of small black bats hung by an old clock placed high above us on the wall of the top landing. The reception hall also led into a series of interconnecting rooms of elaborate proportions, a library, a drawing-room, a long dining-room with french doors.

In the drawing-room we paused to talk by a beautiful white marble fireplace. We listened while Mr Warner talked respectfully and fondly of the better days of the old mansion. He was a Blockley villager who had been a lifelong employee of the former owner of the house, the late Captain Spencer-Churchill. Now he was the bailiff with care of the mansion and oversight of the Northwick estate of 4,000 acres. The deterioration of the house was obviously distressing to him.

The house had in fact been completely empty for just three years, but the process of decay had started long before. Captain Spencer-Churchill had been an eccentric bachelor who lived almost exclusively for his valuable collections of art treasures, old coins and porcelains which he housed in a gallery which formed an extra wing to the house. The gallery had been kept in good order to preserve the collections, but apart from the one room in which the captain spent almost all his time, the rest of the house, some fifty or sixty rooms, had fallen into gradual ruin. There was no mains electricity, no running water, and only one working toilet. An outbreak of dry rot had been discovered and in various parts of the house floors had been ripped up and doors taken off their hinges to examine the fungus – but the problem had not been treated and the dry rot was still creeping through the house.

Mr Warner crossed to one of the large drawing-room windows.

'I'll try and let some light and fresh air into the place,' he said.

He gripped the wooden shutter and gave a pull. There was a loud creaking sound as the shutter came completely off its rusted hinges and crashed on to the floor, along with a cloud of dust, feathers and the stiff bodies of several small birds.

But at that moment a shaft of brilliant sunshine flooded in, piercing the gloom and dispelling the chill dank atmosphere. Was it my imagination, or did the whole house really give a sigh? A sigh of relief, a sigh welcoming the return of light and life to the sleeping rooms.

Then I truly loved the house. In spite of the débris I could tell that once it had been vibrant with life and colour. People had filled the house with talking, singing, laughing, crying. I pictured a group of chattering ladies with fluttering fans and long bright ball gowns sweeping down the staircase into this very room. Life for the World was going to breathe back life into this house again.

Don and Mr Warner stood talking at the window. I slipped from the room. The vague memory of something came into my mind. Didn't God once give a promise to Joshua that he could claim every place that the sole of his foot stood on?

I systematically walked all round the house again, standing in every room, every corridor, every odd little nook and cranny I could find. I laid my hands on the walls and prayed that this house would be ours, to use for God's own work.

All too soon Don and I were shaking hands with Mr Warner again.

'Well, if there's anything else I can help you with ... ?'

He seemed a man to trust and I ventured to tell him something of the rehabilitation work we hoped to do with young addicts in this lovely old house, asking him what he felt the local climate of opinion might be to such a thing happening on their doorstep. Was he shocked? If he was, the warm country face hid it well. His only and obvious concern was for the wellbeing of the house in which he had worked as a man and a boy; the rest, he seemed to suggest by his polite reply, was our business.

However, I knew too well the importance of local opinion. Memories of Turnours Hall flooded back. A local councillor who lived near the hall had made noisy protests at the mention of the word 'addicts', imagining that her two teenage daughters would be unable to walk the streets in safety. This kind of opposition often blocked a planning application and on that occasion my own assurances over the moral and social character of many addicts and the presence of supervision were all in vain. I hoped Blockley would be on our side.

Don and I drove on to our next stop – quite as important as our first one. We had an appointment early that afternoon to see the agent, Mr Thistlethwayte himself, at his office in Chipping Norton.

We drove through the leafy countryside chattering together excitedly. We couldn't stop talking about the house, the plans we were already formulating. And yet there was a new seriousness, a new commitment about our conversation. We were on the threshold of a big adventure, poised. We were almost, but not quite, in business.

Our excited conversation was soon submerged in the

chaotic hubbub of the café we found doing a brisk trade in the centre of Chipping Norton. We stood in the queue of lorry drivers, collected plates of steak and kidney pie and chips and two mugs of tea and elbowed our way to a free table.

'If only we can convince Mr Thistlethwayte!'

'Well, there's the fact of me being a builder, Frank; that'll count for something. I can give guarantees about the standard of renovation and so on. My, what an opportunity; it's going to be a real challenge, getting that house in order!'

So we sat, happily picturing a rosy future. Was this the end of our search, the pot of gold at the rainbow's end? One thing we didn't discuss was the huge sum of money involved, though of course the thought of the finance was always at the back of our minds. But it was something we didn't need to discuss. It went without saying. If God was really going to give us this house he wouldn't leave us without the necessary resources. Money was no inhibiting factor to God.

It was a walk of just a few hundred yards across the town square to the Midland Bank Chambers where Mr Thistlethwayte's office was, and at the appointed time we straightened our ties and made our way there.

Until this moment Mr Thistlethwayte had been just a kindly voice on the end of a telephone, but now here he was standing up to lean over his desk and shake hands with us. He was a man in his late thirties, slightly balding, dressed surprisingly in a tweedy sports jacket. I had left the pinstriped city behind; I reminded myself that this was very much a rural area.

A few generalities exchanged, Mr Thistlethwayte made us feel at ease immediately and opened the way for me to talk about my plans for Northwick Park. I was still feeling overwhelmed with enthusiasm, but I knew I had to temper my enthusiasm with wisdom to speak constructively. And so I began to explain about the real need there was for a home in the country for the young people I wanted to help.

There was, I knew, no model to which I could point. There were drug centres and clinics in many big towns, of course, but at that time no one else had tried to rehabilitate addicts in the country. The work of Life for the World would in every sense be a pioneer project. But Northwick Park was ideally situated for such a wonderful experiment.

Mr Thistlethwayte jotted down notes on the pad in front of him. He asked a few simple questions, and I saw that he was leading up to a few that wouldn't be quite as easy to answer.

'Now, Mr Wilson, do you really have any idea of what is involved practically in taking on such a large residence in such a poor condition?'

Thoughts on this had already been formulating in my mind for some time, and actually seeing Northwick Park had given my vague ideas a more definite form. I had known for some time of other projects which achieved marvellous results using voluntary labour, notably a community effort on the Scottish island of Iona in which volunteers had rebuilt a monastery while there on retreat.

If we were to have a community of young people they needed some kind of occupation – and what better than the ready-made task of restoring the house? I felt the rebuilding work would be an ideal therapy, working alongside the long-term emotional and spiritual support and guidance which we hoped would show positive results.

Even as I spoke the real strength of this idea caught

my imagination. We had seen many dilapidated houses before, and then the decay had been a tremendously daunting obstacle. Far from this, the dilapidation of Northwick Park seemed a great asset. Yes, this house really was different from the rest. God was giving me an insight into how the very work of their hands could be the means of greatly helping in the saving of young lives.

As I expanded on this Don would occasionally offer his own comments, explaining that as a builder and a Life for the World trustee he would personally guarantee that the work would be completed to a high standard.

'Now, as to the matter of finances, Mr Wilson. Could you make some kind of offer to the owners of Northwick Park? No figure has been set by them, but the rent ought to be negotiated around the sum of about, say, £6,000 a year?'

I began, hesitantly, to try to explain as simply as I could how as believing Christians we felt confident that God was able to supply a financial need. I was acutely aware of how strange it must have sounded to someone in the business world. We weren't a big organisation, we had no capital – but we had faith in God.

Mr Thistlethwayte slapped his pen down on his desk and smiled. He stood to his feet, sweeping up all our hopes in the pile of papers he thrust under his arm. The interview was over.

'Well, thank you for coming along, Mr Wilson, Mr Lewis. The decision, of course, doesn't rest with me, but I think I have all the required information to give a full report to the owners, and I shall be in touch with you soon.'

The sun was setting in a ball of red flame as we neared London. It had been a day of making history. Before we parted that evening Don and I prayed together that God truly would provide tremendously for us to have North-wick Park.

It was quite late when I arrived home, a fact that came to me forcefully when I discovered Shirley sitting anxiously at the kitchen table. Oh, why had I been so thoughtless? Here I was tearing around the countryside seemingly having all the excitement, while Shirley as always was left alone all day and all evening. It wasn't the first time I'd come home to find my wife close to tears because of the sheer loneliness of her life. My work was very demanding. She never complained that she was deprived materially and accepted gratefully the meagre house-keeping money I gave her, which she always managed so well. But sometimes the strain of having to share me with so many people was really too much for her.

I tried to tell her about the house, but she was sceptical and I couldn't really blame her. It must have seemed to her that I was continually chasing around after a dream, no matter how much she believed in what I was trying to do.

'Oh, Frank, you've seen so many houses. Why should this one be any different?

'Anyway, while you've been having a day in the country, Audrey's been here. She's in a bad way, Frank, we've got to do something soon.'

I sighed, and decided to file all my excitement about Northwick Park till the next day. Poor Shirley.

'I'm sorry you had to deal with her all alone.'

Audrey was one of our 'bad pennies'. She'd kept in touch with us frequently for two or three years. She had, as I have mentioned, made a commitment to becoming a Christian at Life for the World's very first annual meeting, at the Metropolitan Tabernacle, 1967. But since that time she had drifted around, trying desperately to keep off drugs but not always succeeding. Audrey often turned up on our doorstep and we knew that she was one of the many for whom there was no escape from drugs until she was removed physically from all the places where the temptation to take them was too great. She had reached a crisis point in her life.

I decided to call on one of the Life for the World Council members for help. I rang Mr Sadler who lived in Sussex with his daughter and son-in-law, and he agreed to take her into his home for a while.

The arrangements made, I sank wearily into bed. I'll tell Shirley all about Northwick Park at breakfast, I thought as sleep overtook me.

However, someone else got in first with news that morning.

Our quiet lodger Jack came bouncing down the stairs with an unusually wide grin on an unusually pink face.

'It's me and Meg,' he blurted out. 'We're going to get married!'

Jack took us both by surprise. It had been a whirlwind romance, but we'd never imagined Jack would so quickly get around to proposing to Meg. We were delighted. Meg was a wonderful girl, a student at Mount Herman Missionary College.

Then it really was my turn to tell both Jack and Shirley about my eventful day at Northwick Park. Before long we were speculating on how wonderful it would be if Meg and Jack could move into Northwick Park after their marriage as our first staff members.

'Don't forget,' said Shirley, 'we haven't got Northwick Park yet. And we may not. Perhaps it's just another house to cross off our list.' But even as she said it I could tell that she was beginning to waver, beginning to hope that this after all was the end of our search.

10

My immediate attention was claimed by my preparations for a week I was spending working with a youth camp in Holland. So the next few days passed busily.

Monday morning. I sat in our little front room which doubled as an office or an extra bedroom when necessary, checking my flight details. I was due to leave from London Airport early the next day.

The telephone rang, and I recognised immediately the warm tones of Mr Thistlethwayte. I couldn't help it – my heart began to thump loudly.

'Mr Wilson? I've had a word with the owners about Northwick Park and your proposals.'

There was a long pause while I tried to think of some suitable cool reply but it never came.

'We were wondering if you could come along and see us. The owners would very much like to meet you to-morrow afternoon.'

Careless of any consequences, I agreed. The owners

and their solicitors, explained Mr Thistlethwayte, were meeting in their London office. They would like to discuss coming to some arrangement with me.

The time of 2.30 p.m. was agreed for the next day's appointment. I put down the phone and rushed upstairs, where Shirley was dressing the children. I grandly made my announcement, and, no doubt of it now, even my cautious wife was showing some excitement!

Back in the front room I telephoned friends to arrange to be absent for the opening day of the youth camp in Holland and made all the necessary changes concerning my travelling. Mr Thistlethwayte had urged me to take someone with me to the meeting, either a Life for the World Council member or a solicitor, so I rang Don, but he had other commitments for the following day. He suggested that I contact a solicitor to accompany me.

One of our young voluntary workers, I recalled, was a solicitor's clerk. He had been very helpful drawing up the legal document necessary to register Life for the World as a charitable trust. He had done all this with the permission of his firm and a senior partner, a Mr Young, had checked it through. I decided to ring Mr Young and ask him if he would represent us as a solicitor at the meeting.

Mr Young was free on the following afternoon, though very sceptical when I explained to him about Northwick Park. He cautioned me very soberly on a hundred and one things which could go wrong in an agreement of this nature, but finally agreed to come with me, mainly I think because he thought I was extremely gullible and likely to be taken advantage of!

'Let me do all the talking, Mr Wilson.'

These words summed up his final piece of advice to me as we arrived together at Millbank Towers, where the London offices of the owners were situated. With us were two others – a farming friend interested in the 500 acres of land on the Northwick estate which was up for sale, and a Life for the World supporter who was in the property business. We were doing our best to look official, but the luxurious office suites and the efficient secretaries striding purposefully up and down the carpeted corridors were very intimidating. The lift carried us smoothly and silently up to the seventeenth floor.

'Now, just you remember, Mr Wilson, this could be a very tricky interview. Just don't commit yourself. Let me do all the talking.'

We sat on a row of chairs in a kind of reception area which led into a boardroom. Behind the boardroom door there was a soft murmur of conversation.

At last the door opened, and we stood up to shake hands with a dark-haired middle-aged man who introduced himself as Mr Webster, a lawyer representing the Northwick Park owners. He spoke in undertones which made us feel even more overawed. He led us into the boardroom, a magnificent room with wood panelled walls, deep pile carpet, dominated entirely by an enormous boardroom table, around which were seated six very smartly dressed gentlemen.

The meeting was obviously finalising some points of business, conferring on some matter was coming to a close and papers were being gathered up and put into leather briefcases. Mr Webster motioned to some empty seats along one side of the board table and we sat down.

I instantly recognised Mr Thistlethwayte, who gave me a friendly nod from the other side of the table. None of the others were known to me.

Finally the man who seemed to be chairing the meeting and who I realised was the real owner of Northwick Park, cleared his throat and stood up, asking me to tell them about Life for the World.

Having introduced myself and my three companions I yet again found myself relating the story of my work among addicts and my growing conviction of the need for a rehabilitation centre situated far from the temptations of the drug-taking world. I told them about the conditions I had met with in London trying to contact young addicts on the city's 'heartbreak corner'; I told them about the anguish of the mothers, and the despair of those who had died. I told them how I had watched many young people destroying their bodies and their futures, powerless to do anything of any lasting value to help change their dreadful situations.

They listened without a word. I told them about our little organisation, a penniless band of caring people looking for a house of new beginnings.

'We have no money, but we've a lot of faith. We trust God, and if you would be willing to trust us with your wonderful house at a reasonable rent I know we could rebuild it to the glory of God and to the saving of many young lives.'

I came to an abrupt halt. The silence continued. The men opposite me slowly came to life, exchanging brief glances, and a few words I couldn't catch.

Then the chairman turned to the jovial-looking man sitting next to him and said loudly enough for everyone to hear, 'Well, what do you think, Jim?'

This man smiled and looked across at me.

'Well, Mr Wilson, we have of course already discussed your ideas and after hearing you today it's our wish to do all we can to encourage you and to help the work of Life for the World. It seems from what you've been telling us that plenty of experts have tried and failed to solve the problem of addiction. We think it's about time God was given a chance.'

'Hear, hear,' I heard from one of the others.

Now the chairman spoke.

'We would be willing to rent the mansion to you at a rent of £250 a year. What do you say to that?'

I could feel Mr Young who was sitting next to me grab the edge of his chair and I suddenly realised I hadn't let him say anything, which after all his kindly-meant warnings that I should 'let him do all the talking', seemed a bit unfair. So, hardly realising the real significance of what had just been said about the rent, I gave him a questioning look which suggested that he should reply this time. He looked totally unprepared. He had just lit his pipe and now it was hanging limply from his lips, he was so taken aback by what he had just heard.

He came to his senses and removed his pipe hastily.

'Yes, hmm, that sounds very reasonable, very reasonable, but what kind of lease were you thinking of?'

'Oh, I hadn't thought of anything too hard and fast,' the chairman replied casually.

'Name your terms and we'll be happy to fit in with anything you want to do.'

Gradually the true facts began to dawn on me. We were being offered Northwick Park at a ridiculously low rent – less than five pounds a week! Mr Young's worst fears were definitely not being realised.

Mr Young and the others began to work out a few of the necessary details for drawing up a lease and I allowed myself the luxury of sinking into my own private world, in which my thoughts revolved around the tremendous feelings of praise and thanksgiving towards God which were welling up inside me. God was in that room. He had taken the decisions around the board table. He was the

God of the impossible and today I had proved it again for myself.

'Mr Wilson, Mr Wilson . . . did you hear?'

I came down to earth with a jolt.

'I'm sorry, were you saying something to me?'

It was the chairman. Did I think a twenty-one-year lease would suit us?

It would; it sounded marvellous!

'What about the insurance premiums?' Mr Young was asking.

'You realise that the Life for the World trustees have no capital. They might be able to raise the rent, but supposing they can't pay the premiums on the lease?' he added.

The reply was instant.

'Well, the estate will pay to keep the mansion insured and will charge Life for the World in arrears.'

It seemed that every objection the solicitor put up was generously dealt with. The meeting was drawing to a close.

'We do hope that this will encourage you in your work,' said the chairman. 'When do you want to move in?'

'I hadn't thought about that yet,' I replied.

'You won't want to commit yourself until the lease is properly signed,' interrupted Mr Young.

'I don't think you need worry about the formalities,' said the chairman. 'We are as anxious to do things properly as you are, but we have no objection to you moving into the house before the lease is signed.'

Mr Webster showed us out and walked with us to the lift. Down we went, seventeen floors. But it was very different to our ride up. Mr Young was deep in thought.

'I've never known anything quite like this before,' he said with a puzzled frown as we stepped out into the busy

London street. 'I am bound to say that you have been offered a very fair and advantageous agreement.'

And for a solicitor I didn't think that was a bad expression of approval!

It was my second visit to Northwick Park. Now as we turned into the drive and eagerly caught the first glimpse of the mansion through the trees any possible feelings of detachment melted away. I was no longer an onlooker. The agreement was signed. The house was ours.

With me were Life for the World Council member John Noble and Peter Ward, a Christian photographer who was going to help us with publicity material about the house which was going to be sent to our prayer partners, all those who now regularly supported us with prayer and gifts of money.

This time it was I who led the way through the overgrown weeds to the back door. As arranged, Mr Warner had left a key under a brick by the side of the door. Again the great key turned in the rusty lock and I stepped inside the damp and gloomy servants' quarters. It felt good. Like coming home.

I made my way to the grander side of the house, crossed the bottom of the grand central circular staircase and into the main reception hall where the huge main door stood.

It was rusted shut. Soon, though, it would be opened, opened to welcome many. I stood and looked at its massive wooden panels. There had been many who had laughed when I had said that one day we'd have a house. My thoughts went back to that early meeting in Dr Chapple's clinic when I'd been suddenly confronted with addicts and staff waiting to hear my ideas. 'One day God is going to give me a house.' That's what I'd told them.

Someone had shouted out 'Where's the bread (money) coming from?' Well, God had kept his promises, all of them, and he was going to provide in every way for his work here. God was going to open this door. I leaned against the rusted lock and felt very secure. I closed my eyes and whispered 'Thank you God for all you are going to do in the years to come in this, your house ...'

11

The enormous crash on my study door startled me. Before I was able to say 'Come in' the door burst open and in hurtled our liaison probation officer.

Did this mean trouble? We had been at Northwick Park for over two years now and Mr Barter had been our liaison probation officer for most of that period, making regular visits to supervise the rehabilitation of the handful of our residents who were with us under a probation order. We had exchanged only the most basic pleasantries and sometimes hostilities with regard to particular clients of his. Mr Barter could never understand these crazy unprofessional Christians who had turned up on his patch and started poking their noses into drug addiction. I felt he dismissed us as do-gooders, misdirected amateurs.

I was at a loss to understand this present outburst, and looked up at him anxiously. But suddenly the serious professional face was wreathed in smiles.

'Put it there, Mr Wilson!' So I put it there, a little

amazed to find him offering his hand in such an un-characteristic manner! He shook mine energetically and began to unravel the mystery.

He had just been to see Tony, one of his clients and one of our newest residents.

Mr Barter's voice was full of wonder.

'The last time I spoke to that boy, why, he was one of the most mixed-up, confused, lost young people I've ever dealt with in all my years as a probation officer. But today, well, not only does he appear to be a completely changed young man, with a new mind and a completely new motivation towards life, but he's even got the cheek to try to tell me what's wrong with my life and how I should get sorted out!

'Well, Mr Wilson, if ever I had doubts about the effectiveness of your work they've all been dispelled as I've talked with Tony today.'

The conversation that followed marked the beginning of a new and rewarding friendship. As Mr Barter left with a friendly wave I made my way to the office on the ground floor, where I knew Tony C. was working that day.

'Tony, whatever have you done to Mr Barter?'

Tony beamed. 'I just told him about how Jesus has changed me,' he answered simply.

And what a change there had been in Tony C.! He had come to us following several years of heavy addiction to morphine and his mind badly affected by much use of LSD. It had taken a lot of love and understanding to begin to get through to him at all. Often as I counselled him he would break off in mid-sentence with a bewildered expression on his face and a darkness in his eyes.

'It's no use, it's all gone. I can't remember anything of what you've been saying.'

108

At times he would come looking for me, looking for some release from the evil thoughts and dreadful fears which constantly bombarded his mind. I would pray for God to heal him, to eradicate the memories of the past and repair the damage to his mind which doctors had said was beyond medical help. For a long time he was very unwell and despaired, terrified that the distortion of LSD might be permanent and that he would lead a haunted life.

But slowly, as we told him more and more about Jesus the Healer, he showed signs of positive response. The nightmares grew less, he grew increasingly able to remember our names and to hold simple short conversations. He began to hope and to believe himself that God really was changing him, renewing him.

The real breakthrough began in a seemingly insignificant way.

'I have decided that God wants me to paint this cornice,' said Tony as he led me into the main drawing-room.

I looked up at the elaborate cornice which ran entirely round the walls of our beautiful early-Victorian drawing-room. The plasterwork of intricate leaves and fleur-de-lis had been truly exquisite, but it had crumbled in several places and the colouring was gone. When we had begun the restoration of this lovely room experts had estimated that a professional artist would charge an enormous sum to restore, paint and regild the cornice.

Tony was the last person I would have thought capable of attempting such a task and I tried to tell him so as gently as I could.

'You've no experience of doing anything like this, have you?'

'No, not now. But I will have after I've finished this, and this is what God wants me to do.

109

'You see, I need something important to concentrate on, and I thought that if I could do this job, and nothing else, really concentrate on it, well, I believe that God will use this to heal me, even if it takes me the rest of my life.'

I laughed as I looked down at our little Michaelangelo. Already a miracle had happened. He was a young man who had been down to the very depths of degradation, crime and humiliation of every kind. Now he wanted to paint a cornice for Jesus! I watched him climb the step-ladder determinedly.

And for the next four months apart from mealtimes and chapel services I never saw him anywhere else except perched on the top of his ladder. Propped among his tools was a pocket-sized New Testament. He would read a few verses to himself, and paint a few inches, read a few verses, paint a few inches.

It really was a labour of love. At first progress was painfully slow. But as the cornice came to life with his carefully chosen colours and gold leaf, so Tony came to life, too. And as the project neared completion Tony's mind took dramatic strides towards wholeness.

'It's finished!' he announced one day, knocking on my study door. We walked together to the drawing-room, where other residents were putting final touches to the redecoration of the rest of the room. The cornice with its gleaming gold leaf was the crowning glory of the room. But more wonderful to see was the confident smiling young man who stood beside me.

It was Tony who was responsible for a very important stage in the embryo work of our centre.

'The Lord has set me free from addiction to drugs, but what about addiction to nicotine?' Tony asked, coming into my study one day and placing an opened packet of cigarettes and a box of matches on my desk.

'I think it's wrong; I feel I should give up cigarettes. And I want you to help me,' said Tony.

Well, I thought to myself as I stared up into his earnest face; well. He was right, of course. Nicotine was no less an addictive drug than heroin or LSD. But I had always felt I would be asking far too much of the boys to abandon what was, after all, a socially acceptable habit.

Tony left, assured of my support and help, and I sat back in my chair to think. This young man's willingness to abandon cigarettes, his desire, even, that I should enforce on him a 'no smoking' rule, made me reflect seriously about our rehabilitation work. Until this time life had been pretty easy going at Northwick Park in the sense of there being a relatively unstructured day with no real rules. Boys were not restricted except in giving up all drugs. They came and went freely.

Would it be better to have a more structured approach, with certain rules to be obeyed? Firstly, I had to see how Tony fared in his personal 'no smoking' battle.

I had to admit that I didn't think Tony's resolution would last. He made a calm announcement at tea-time that he intended to give up smoking and explained why. The rest of the residents laughed and joked, and the staff members smiled sceptically.

But in the days that followed, Tony maintained a calm silence, sitting apparently unperturbed in the midst of a crowd of smokers – who meanwhile began to feel more and more guilty!

Some resorted to trying to badger Tony into smoking again. But he was determined. And finally it was the other residents who began to crack – as one by one they came to me and added to a growing pile of cigarette packets in my desk drawer.

Not that this was the end of the matter. Far from it.

The others were not able to withstand the temptation of smoking as well as Tony did. The procession reversed itself, as one by one residents crept back to my study to beg for the return of their cigarettes!

The feelings of guilt and friction continued and finally smoking was the subject of a heated community meeting. Tony C. stood to his feet.

'Look, there's only one way to settle this. You've got to make a rule about no smoking and keep us to it,' he said dramatically, pointing at me.

The rest nodded their agreement.

'Oh, no,' I said. 'I'm not going to be caught like that! If I make the rule I shall be the scapegoat, you'll accuse me of forcing the rule on you all. If you want a "no smoking" rule then you must all make it and keep it.'

'Listen,' said Tony C., joining the discussion for the first time. 'I didn't give up smoking to be sanctimonious. I wasn't trying to be better than everyone else. I did it because I really feel it's inconsistent for us to claim we are delivered from drugs and yet continue to smoke. Let's face it, some of you are far more hung up over losing cigarettes than losing your junk. And if it's that serious it needs dealing with, doesn't it?'

Tony had put the case for no smoking in a way I couldn't have, and I was thrilled and deeply grateful to God for him. And so, after a trial period of twenty-four hours in which to think it all over, the residents brought in their own 'no smoking' rule – adhered to by Life for the World ever since. And this one rule was the very important basis for a whole structure of rules that grew out of our experiences. Increasingly since that time Life for the World has demanded a high degree of personal commitment from all the community – and that commitment has borne great fruit over the years.

Tony's story is forever immortalised by that cornice. And as the years passed I was able to walk the house and grounds and see many, many more faces represented in the restoration work. The painting of the ornamental pillars in the entrance hall reminds me of Chris, the rebuilt kitchen wall of Phil, other carefully plastered walls of Alan and Trevor. I think of David and Paul as I turn on each light switch, the new windows remind me of Mike and Roger. Dennis and John come to mind as I look at the fresh paintwork, also Tim and Andy, Chris and Bill and many others. The new tiles on the roof recall David and Lionel, the carefully tended lawns and gardens speak of two more Davids, John, Tony, Mike. The stables remind me of Peter and John, Gus and Alan and many others who turned their hands to farmwork. The printing press set up in the stable block brings back memories of Roy and Bob, Hugh, Allan, Terry, Bryan, Keith and Peter. In the kitchen I think of all those who slaved over a hot stove for the benefit of the community – among them Chris, Phil, Colin, Jonty.

The house tells a thousand stories of those who came and went. And those who prayed and gave. We gratefully received thousands of pounds worth of gifts from companies and individuals – a central heating system, electrical goods, sanitary ware, paints and wallpapers. The work was wonderfully achieved by the co-operation of the resident ex-addicts, staff members and short-term voluntary workers.

The restoration of the mansion and the restoration of many scores of broken young lives went marvellously hand in hand. We saw miracles take place in the lives of individuals. And often tremendous things would happen to show that God was blessing the house itself as well as those who lived in it.

Perhaps the most wonderful example of this was the incident of the dry rot. Yes, we knew when we took the house over that dry rot had broken out in parts of it. But it was only later that we realised how severe the outbreak was. A specialist firm estimated that it would cost £15,000 to eradicate the fungus that was creeping through the house and make good the damage.

This discovery, in the difficult early days of our time at Northwick Park, was daunting to say the least. At that stage, with an annual income of £3,000 the target of £15,000 seemed impossible. We decided to investigate the possibility of doing the work ourselves and the owners were willing to give us £2,000 towards the cost.

Well, we knew a Jesus who was able to turn five loaves and two fishes into a feast for a multitude. Could £2,000 in his hands be enough to do £15,000 worth of work?

It was Shirley who prepared the way for the miracle. Late one night she was reading her Bible when I was getting ready for bed.

'Look, Frank! Read this. God can heal walls!'

I read the verses in the Old Testament that she pointed out to me. It was an obscure passage detailing methods for dealing with the diseased walls of houses by prayer and the laying on of hands.

'Well, if walls can be healed with prayer, why not a whole house?' she said. 'Why not our house? This dry rot is a sort of disease.'

Shirley wasn't one given to emotional speculation and I was prepared to summon my faith to test it out. I studied the chapter again.

'Let's hope it works,' I said, 'because I don't think the owners would appreciate the kind of drastic measures we'd have to take otherwise!'

'What do you mean?' she asked.

'Well,' I laughed, 'the Bible says that if prayer didn't have any effect the diseased walls were to be burned down!'

Feeling somewhat self-conscious I systematically toured the house early the next day, laying my hands on every part of the walls and roof known to be affected by the dry rot. 'Lord Jesus,' I prayed, 'we ask you to perform a miracle. We have no money to repair this house and we claim your promise for healing as given in this passage of your Word.'

It was a few weeks later that I had a letter from the managing director of a firm producing chemicals for eradicating dry rot, in reply to some enquiries I'd made. The managing director was very interested in Life for the World's work and was sending his chief engineer to inspect the extent of the dry rot damage.

So one wet and grey morning the engineer arrived and disappeared for several hours into the labyrinth of corridors and roof space of the mansion.

There was a look of utter bewilderment on his face as he sat down in my study to give me the results of his investigation.

'It's very strange,' he said. 'Very strange. You have had a massive outbreak of rot. But quite suddenly at some point it has literally stopped growing, stopped dead. It should be spreading around the entire house, but it's lifeless.'

I could hardly believe my ears. What a lack of faith I'd shown. It was a miracle, God really had healed the house of dry rot.

'In all my working experience I'd never seen anything like this,' the engineer went on. 'So it's not going to be a difficult thing to deal with at all. You can easily do the work yourselves. Just remove the heavily damaged parts and spray the area with the chemicals we can supply, just to be on the safe side.'

That evening as I walked around the house saying good-night to the boys in our care I couldn't lose the tremendous sense of wonder at the greatness of God. In every circumstance of need that I had taken to him since our arrival at Northwick Park, he had answered beyond the extent of all my dreams.

12

'Mr Wilson? It's Roy! Remember me?'

It wasn't a very good line, but there was no mistaking Roy's rough London accent.

'Of course. How could I forget you!' I laughed.

How could I forget any of the boys we took into our care? By the time they left they were part of the North-wick family which within a few years numbered several hundred.

I remembered Roy sitting down in a corner of a room for hours on end with a broken expression on his face. He had come to us having spent most of the previous ten years in and out of a prison cell. He had been heavily addicted to barbiturates and like Tony his mind was shattered.

Roy was the first resident to work in our printing press, and the staff member in charge there patiently taught him the printer's trade. How thrilling it was when Roy left to take up a career in printing and began to attend and become involved in a church of loving, caring people.

'Well, guess what? Wanna come to a wedding? Yes, it's right! I've got a smashing girl, Mr Wilson.'

Thus Roy announced his engagement, and I was thrilled.

It was wonderful to hear all the success stories, I reflected as I put down the phone. For instance, Tony had gone on to Bible College, where he was to gain high honours and meet Elizabeth, who would become his lovely wife. Together they were destined to go to Valetta, Malta's capital, where Tony would become pastor of a little mission.

Sometimes, of course, the phone brought details of those whose very success was tinged with sadness, like that of Jackie.

We had left John and Jackie in the flat at St Leonard's, but one day Gordon Hunt was again on the phone. This time his voice was filled with sadness.

'It seems beyond belief,' Gordon said. 'John is dead!' he choked on the words. Death is no stranger to a minister, but the meaningless, needless death of an addict affects all of us deeply in our hearts. So many times these young people had died in my presence, yet like Gordon I could never get used to it, the sharpness, the pain, the bitterness.

I found my voice and asked a question, dreading the answer even as I asked.

'Why? How?'

'He took an overdose of heroin, he left a message to say that Jackie stood a better chance of making it without him. He cared about the children so much that he thought they would all do better without the added burden of his addiction.' There was a moment's silence and then he added, 'I've been asked to take the funeral, I think you had better come along, I don't think I want to face this on my own.'

My mind was far away, already questioning, where had I gone wrong this time? Only a week ago I had been with John, a hopeful, positive John and Jackie. Why had John done this, why? There was still so much I didn't understand.

'Will you come?' It was Gordon.

'Come? Come where?' I asked needlessly.

'To John's funeral, I feel I need your moral support.'

'Oh, forgive me,' I said. 'Yes, sure I'll be there. Just let me know the details; I'll be there.'

Gordon told me the date and time. No church service, just at the cemetery chapel. He told me that Jackie was in a terrible state and had buried herself in a cocoon of drugs. Since she had found John, she hadn't returned to sanity and the children had had to be taken into care. She was in great need.

When I put the phone down all I could do was fall on my knees and weep! I felt a mixture of guilt and sorrow. If only I had insisted that they come to Northwick when I was with them. Only a week previously I had received a call from Jackie asking if I would meet them and take them as a couple into Northwick Park. We had met in a Lyons' Tea Shop at Charing Cross and they had filled me in with the past twelve months. Since the dreadful scene in their flat in St Leonard's things had gone from bad to worse, they were destroying themselves and their children, and they knew they had to do something about their lives before the authorities took the children away. Jackie had done most of the talking; if we would have them they were prepared for the children to be taken care of while they sorted their lives out. Although silent during most of the conversation, John was positive, or so I thought; I think he was silently planning this all along. When I asked him what he thought about it, he would say, 'I will do whatever's best for Jackie!' and he meant it.

I wanted them to return with me right away, but there were too many things to do. The furniture to store, the children to look after. How many times have I found that addicts will put off the day when they actually take the positive necessary action – there are always so many things to do. How often I have heard a desperate young man say, 'I'll come next week, I have a few things to sort out!' How seldom they actually arrive.

I felt the loss of John so deeply. I had come to love and respect this quiet, patient man. He had so much to offer. Oh how pointless his death seemed. Jackie needed her strong silent husband; could it be that he simply couldn't be strong any more? I would never know now.

It was raining in a steady drizzle. I had arrived just in time to slip into the back of the chapel as Gordon commenced the short funeral service. The people were familiar and Jackie sat at the front dressed in black with John's parents. I was surprised to see so many people there, many from the church. Everything seemed so final, no going back, no fresh start, not for John at least – would there be for Jackie?

John was laid to rest in a simple grave, we stood round the place as Gordon said the closing words of the service: ' . . . in sure and certain hope of the resurrection of the dead . . . ' If only two weeks ago John had seen that life was available to him then, eternal life and a full life now! If only all the young people like him could have grasped the message of hope Christ was giving!

As the mourners climbed into the cars I tried to say something to Jackie, a word of comfort, or question? I don't know, but she was too lost in her own thoughts, or was it the effect of drugs, to even notice me. She disappeared in a big black car with a few friends trying to comfort her and was gone out of sight as the rain came down like a curtain pronouncing the finale of a grim act.

Suddenly there were no more people, I was alone with John, and he too was gone beyond recall. I prayed, briefly, then ran for the shelter of my car and hopefully Gordon's home.

Events were confusing in the following days. I remained in the area and called our faithful nurse Christine to come to help Jackie if she could. Jackie was in a state of confusion and under the influence of drugs. The children were in a local authority home and Jackie was merely existing from day to day. It was clear that the only thing that mattered to her were her children and now even they had been snatched from her. The court had told her if she got her life sorted out and could provide a stable home for the children, they would be returned to her, but not before. She was told if she returned with me and Christine for help, the children would eventually join her. Poor Jackie was so angry and confused and her reckless drinking and taking drugs made her even less of a candidate for responsible motherhood.

Two days after John's funeral Gordon and I took her to the foster home to see the children. She had been drinking and using drugs, but managed to compose herself for the most important event of her life, her children. She managed reasonably well until it was time to leave and then everything went wrong.

'I want my children, why can't I have them?' she screamed. Somehow the combination of grief and drugs had removed from Jackie the truth of the matter, why her children were not with her. She was convinced that we were all in the conspiracy to steal her children from her. It was an ugly scene and eventually we had to physically force her into the car and rush her away in tears, and as we went she accused us of stealing her children and all kinds of other things.

That evening Christine slept in Jackie's home and I stayed with Gordon. We had carried her up the stairs of her flat in a very undignified way – she had taken a lot of Mandrax and was sound asleep five minutes after leaving the children's home.

How we prayed that night – could Jackie ever now be changed? We prayed believing that she would.

Twenty-four hours later we arrived with Jackie at Northwick. Most of the journey she had been silent and sleeping. She came reluctantly, but it seemed the only way she would ever see her children again.

Jackie blamed me and Gordon for everything. She was convinced that we had conspired with the authorities to take her children away. Poor girl she was so confused and lost, nothing I could say would alter her opinion.

Jackie's time with us was brief and bitter. She was too aggressive and had so many devious habits. She still drank and took drugs which she brought in with her. She gave some to the new male members of the community and caused much pain. We prayed with her and cared as much as we could, but oh, how aware we became of our limitations.

One sunny morning Jackie left us. We didn't know where she would go or to whom. She was obsessed with her desire to get her children back. Her departure, like her stay, was very bitter and we were only enemies to her, not the friends we so longed to be.

That wasn't the end of Jackie! A year later she phoned and spoke to my wife. She had been accepted by Phoenix House, a new, secular therapeutic community.

'Will you tell Frank Wilson,' she snarled, ' . . . that I'm off drugs and all right – my children are with me, he said I'd never make it on my own – well I have, no thanks to him!'

Shirley said afterwards that the phone nearly disintegrated in her hand. She ventured to reply to Jackie's triumphant statement. 'I'm sure Frank will be glad to hear that Jackie; I'll tell him.'

'Umph!' was the reply. 'I doubt that he'll be pleased!' and that was all we heard for more than two years. Then out of the blue a postcard came from her. She was in Ireland and doing very well, helping other addicts. Then a phone call; this time I was in.

Jackie told me how she was, all was well. She really was off drugs and a new person. Had this really happened without God?

'By the way, Frank,' she said softly. 'I guess God didn't forget me after all eh? I think your prayers did work after all!'

With this she said good-bye, but I knew that after many years of sorrow and loss Jackie had come home to Jesus, in her own time and the Good Shepherd had patiently sought for his lost sheep and not rejected her even when she had forsaken him. He was bringing her home rejoicing and giving her complete healing.

13

So by phone and letter the news came to us. There was one letter in particular that started a story which was to affect me deeply – the story of Paul.

The letter was full of anguish: I couldn't put it down. I read and re-read it; each line poured out the pain, the unique pain of a mother who had been told that her son was going to die. 'They tell me that he has less than a year to live, but I refuse to give up hoping that he will seek for help, so many people are praying for him. I will not believe that God will let my son die! Paul is more fortunate than most, people care and are praying for him!'

Paul's mother had lived in hope for several years that he would one day stop using the damaging, soul-destroying drugs he was so bitterly addicted to and find a cure, an answer to his endless quest for life. Doctors and probation officers had given up in despair. Paul himself had given up. There were no answers, no end to the search for reality he had so earnestly been looking for; he was prepared even for death which was undeniably reaching out for him as his young body of only eighteen years sank slowly into a pit of despair. Yet Paul's mother, the writer of the letter I now held in my hand, was a woman of faith and no matter what scientific opinion may be, she refused to believe that Paul could die just like that.

This young boy's mother had been writing to me since the early days of Northwick Park, always hoping that one day Paul, an incurable amphetamine addict, would respond to her pleas to contact me. Until now all seemed to have failed. Her son had very little time left, he was dying, his body seeming unable to keep up the effort of living any longer and he still refused help. It somehow sounds 'corny' when talked about by cynics, but a mother's prayers and love *can* work miracles. Paul had a praying mother who held on to her son's life by faith alone!

As my eyes traced the agonised words of the letter, they fastened on the last paragraph for the fourth or fifth time. 'Paul came home last night, he was in a dreadful state and although he seemed unable to talk or take anything in, he did say that he would come down to see Northwick Park some day. I know it's only a faint hope but at least he's willing to think about it.'

To me, at that early stage of our rehabilitation work, Paul was just one of scores whom we seemed to hear of and yet never see, because they never quite made it to the house – often they died, tragically and needlessly. I had no reason to think that this one would be any different or that his association with us would be significant in any way in my own understanding of the need, the heartbreaking need of the addict. Yet Paul was to be used of God as my instructor in trust and love; through this hitherto unknown and incurable young addict God was going to teach me the most precious lesson of all, how to trust those whom I cared for and how to receive from them what they can give best of all – love. It isn't easy to know when to put your trust in an addict; his whole life is a fabric of lies and deceit. Letting loved ones down is of no consequence at all when your very existence hangs in the balance and the only reality is a needle or a pill. Addicts think nothing of taking and giving nothing in return; the law of the jungle rules. I put the letter away in a file after writing yet another reply in which I tried to reassure Paul's mother. We were ready when Paul was, but I doubted that I would ever hear anything from Paul except the same sad news that he had died. How wrong I was I was very soon to find out.

Those early days at Northwick were days of learning. We seemed to make so many mistakes, but looking back, I realise that we learned so much from them. Our staff, too numerous to talk of much in this story, turned over rapidly. It was hard for Shirley and me to really relax with the sincere and willing, yet young workers we had. Already several had left us, discovering the cost of caring too great. There was a certain 'glamour', though heaven knows, I never saw it, in working with addicts. Enthusiasm was always high as new people joined us. Someone only had to tell me, 'The Lord has called me!' and I would believe them and take them on to our already overstretched staff payroll. Somehow though, I could never understand why these keen people treated God's work like a slimming diet, beginning with such enthusiasm and giving up so easily and often with such bitterness and bad feeling left behind them. I began to despair that love and loyalty could ever be found in the hearts of those who came. God was planning on teaching me a lesson and one I would never forget and it came in the form of a skinny, pale-faced long-haired youth whose name was Paul.

One cold morning in February one of our staff workers walked into my office and placed a letter in front of me. It was from the Coventry City Probation and After-Care Service. On the top of the letter was neatly underlined the name Paul Tandy. I remembered the letters I had received from that caring mother; well who would have believed it. Paul's Probation Officer wanted to bring him down for a visit and an interview to become a resident. 'I don't like the sound of him!' stated my colleague; 'he looks like a lost cause.' 'Yes,' I said, 'I know, he probably is. I've been sharing this lad's sorrow with his parents by letter, but let him come, if he makes it.'

Paul did make it and he stayed only long enough to slip into the toilets at Northwick and take a massive dose of drugs. The staff member in charge of the interview never even bothered to introduce him to me, he was so stoned and uncommunicative. The Probation Officer and Paul beat a hasty, and for the P.O. red-faced, retreat.

I decided that was the last Northwick would see of Paul and as the staff of the time and I discussed it, it was obvious nobody wanted to see such a difficult person back in those sensitive and formative days of the work. It seemed impossible that Paul would try again; it was too good to be true that he had come so far as to even visit us at all. My mind dismissed the matter and sadly the file was closed. But you see, God had plans for Paul and like it or not I was going to have to deal with this young man.

The weeks went by and no more was heard from Paul until late one afternoon just a few weeks before Easter, John, one of our new and inexperienced staff members, buzzed me on the internal telephone: 'Remember that boy Paul Tandy? Well he wants to come back for an interview. I think he's a bit of a non-starter; could be a waste of time!' How strange; my heart leapt for joy, 'Thank God!' I said. 'Let him come; I'll talk to him this time!'

Paul was to be given a second chance, and if I did but know it, so was I.

He arrived early one morning the following week. This time the Probation Officer had made sure Paul had no drugs on him, though I suspect he had plenty in him to fortify him for the trip. One of the residents was given the job of showing him around the house. This was an early practice of ours to show a would-be resident the house and to let him hear the rules from one who was already used to them. Tony C had already helped us to create the 'no smoking' rule and this along with ten or more other demands was explained to Paul.

Eventually, the moment I suppose I had unconsciously been a long time waiting for, arrived; Paul was ready to see me. First of all John, our staff member who had seen him previously, came into the room. 'He seems no different; he's very arrogant and there's a brick wall around him miles high!' he said. He was still remembering the abortive first visit. 'I really don't think he wants to come; he's got some idea that he's doing this for his parents' sake and his girlfriend who he says is going to marry him when he gets off drugs – not a very good reason really!'

John's words sounded so accurate; could we help this helpless young man? All the signs so far were negative.

'Bring him in, John,' I asked and said a silent prayer for guidance and wisdom. I was so green at this job, how was I to know what to look for? I wanted this to be so right, and I felt so useless!

The door had opened softly as I had been lost in my prayer. Paul stood there unannounced, and I, expecting John to have brought him in, was taken by surprise. For what seemed an eternity we stared at each other.

Paul was thin, very thin, and his long hair which reached down below his chest almost completely obscured his face. I was just aware of blue-grey eyes looking at me from beneath the security of the hair covering; did I notice a hint of mischief, clean fun in those eyes? My eyes travelled up and down the skinny form. His mock-leather coat clung to scrawny arms and elbows stuck out in protest. His black baggy trousers were full of holes and he trembled, a strange involuntary tremble through his whole body.

'Oh, hello,' I said, breaking the silence, 'I'm Frank Wilson.'

'I'm Paul Tandy,' he replied jauntily. Somehow I was aware of an instant rapport between us and Paul confirmed this by giving me a toothy grin, tossing his head so that the covering of hair momentarily revealed all of his face. I liked him and also felt a strong sense of compassion for this broken young man. I invited him to sit down and as I walked round from my desk he slumped into one of the upright chairs with feet stretched out in front and his chin resting on his chest so that the hair once more provided a hideout from under which he could inspect me without feeling exposed. He remained in that position for most of the interview and I never really did see his face until he got up to leave and once more tossed the hair away from his eyes.

In the half-hour or so that I talked to Paul, I got to know the heart of this needy young man very well. He knew he had very little time left to live and really he did care, very much. He cared about his mother and father, he was aware of the pain he was causing them; he was also aware of his mother's faith, having been brought up in a Christian atmosphere and having attended church services until the age of fourteen with his parents. Yet this

129

very background which should be the answer now to his need was also the barrier to him accepting a spiritual answer. He was cynical about Christianity, he was 'in to' many forms of eastern religion, he wrote poetry, sad soulful poetry which expressed his own longing for something real.

He used amphetamines in a particularly nasty way. The inside of his body was breaking up and the marks on his young face already revealed the losing battle going on inside. Sometimes he lived with his girlfriend, other times with drug users in their dungeon-like pads, or he slept out in an open field or in a nearby grave-yard. Often he would wake in the morning on the verge of death from exposure, and stumble to the office of his doctor, Probation Officer or on occasions to his home. His mother, who loved him dearly couldn't, for the sake of the other children, allow him in the house for any length of time, but she would at least feed him and wash and mend his pathetic clothing. Paul was one hundred per cent addict and he was as good as dead.

Strangely, as we talked, filling up the thirty minutes with details about ourselves, a deep understanding grew between us. I knew Paul longed to be free, but his stubborn will wouldn't yield. He knew we could help him; that in the protection of this old house, he could hide without drugs to obscure his real self or the covering of hair to close his face to the outside world. He wanted to come to us and both of us wanted to learn from the other. Soon we were smiling at each other and Paul was laughing, hollow and without much humour, but his laughter revealed a willingness to change.

'I do want to come,' he kept on saying, 'and I believe this is the only place where there is any hope for me.' Truth was beginning to dawn on Paul, but the light had barely shone on me; yet, for me there was much more to come from this young teacher.

I stood up and walked over to Paul's still slumped form in the chair. He jumped up, startling me. 'You can come right away,' I said, regaining my composure.

'I've got a few things to arrange,' he said, 'I'll come next Monday.'

'Okay . . . ' and taking a deep breath and clutching a handful of his long hair I said ' . . . and you can get a haircut before you come.' I smiled, knowing that this was going to be the crunch for him!

'What!' he actually became animated. 'Cut my hair? I've got an ambition to grow it down to the small of my back!'

'Not if you come here,' I said.

Paul smiled ruefully and then with that now familiar toss of the head and with a twinkle in his eyes said, 'All right! I half expected that.' And as an afterthought, 'It'll please my dad; he's been trying to get me to cut it for years!'

I said good-bye to Paul and his companion after arranging for his admission, and as I watched the car go down the drive I knew we would be seeing Paul again.

'I hope you are right about him!' my doubtful colleague was by my side again. I didn't know, I only felt inside that this was what God wanted, and I wanted it too!

Paul's early days with us were uneventful; he worked with the other residents in the gardens under the watchful and prayerful eye of our new farm manager, John Dean. Paul hadn't a clue how to do practical work and was useless at anything to do with farm work. I would often sit at my study window and watch him trying to push a cart full of garden waste; he was still skinny and very weak. He would

131

take the slope at a run and after a few steps collapse with exhaustion, but for all that he was willing.

Paul found rules irksome and would spend any amount of time arguing about this rule or that. Our newly appointed nurse was at her wits end to know how to handle him and a sort of love-hate relationship existed between them. But the times with Paul I remember best of all were at lunch breaks or late afternoons when work was done and he would perch on top of the post and rail fence at the front of the house, sometimes in conversation with the other residents and often alone. He used to tell me that nature was so wonderful to him and the poet in him would be inspired on his lofty vantage point. Yet he still remained aloof, especially to any attempt on my part to get through to him on spiritual matters: God seemed to have nothing for Paul, he felt no need of his help and every time the conversation got round to Jesus, he would change the topic. Once, as he followed me into a group meeting, he said, 'You know it would be very easy for me to pretend to be converted, then everyone would accept me!' I replied: 'Not so easy, Paul; I would know, and God would know, and what's more you would know!'

'What's the difference,' he said, 'if I pretend to be a Christian, and I was brought up on the Bible, no one would know . . . ' he trailed off and looked thoughtful. 'If I die, as everyone says I will, it'll be interesting, won't it?' He looked thoughtful and invited no further comment.

The days and weeks went by. Paul became more part of the centre, but remained aloof from any spiritual influence. I longed for him to seek for Christ because I knew this would be the only answer to his restless search.

The burdens of staff coming and going continued. The problems of simply leading the work in those pioneer days were growing. As I became more experienced, the burdens got heavier, not lighter. I don't say this to complain, but simply to set the scene for the most wonderful experience I was shortly to know. I often used to long to find loyal, understanding workers and committee members. People seemed to only think of themselves and their problems. I was swiftly learning that good workers were going to be hard to find and this was a great weight.

Easter was fast approaching, the third one in our new centre. In the previous weeks I had been unable to spend much time with Paul, but he seemed to be just the same. Still sitting on his fence gazing at nature, still sitting on the spiritual fence, unable, or unwilling to commit himself. Then it happened. Paul found Christ, on Easter Day.

Each Sunday we held a small service in our little chapel, which in reality was the old seventeenth-century servants' dining-hall converted into a meeting room. On Easter Sunday we held a service of praise and I preached about the blood of Jesus, his Cross and his Love, of the empty tomb and life everlasting.

As the service ended and the chapel emptied, I sat at the little organ and played. Soon the room was empty, but for one staff member and Paul, yes Paul! He sat with his head hung low, seemingly meditating or listening to the organ. I could hear nothing at first, then softly, barely audible above the organ's music, I heard the sound of crying, of deep sobbing. Was it John, the remaining staff member, surely it couldn't be Paul? I turned round to look and there was Paul, still in the same position, but with his body shaking and rocking to and fro. I stopped playing and walked across to him. As I put my hand on his shoulder he erupted into a great heart-rending sobbing and the floor became a pool of tears under his feet.

'Paul, I've told you that Jesus loves you, you know the

Gospel so well by now, do you want to ask Jesus into your heart?'

The head, still supporting a long mop of hair, even after the approved cut, nodded urgently. Then, without waiting he fell to his knees, still weeping, and between the sobs asked God to take control of his life and to make him into a new creature. The battle was over, the victory was won. Paul became a child of God in that instant; he was born all over again; the search was at an end; now he could begin to live.

John was softly thanking God in the background. I was rejoicing, we were all rejoicing. Suddenly Paul looked up at me, smiling through his tears and flinging his arms around me – he was home and safe and he knew it!

The story doesn't end there, not quite!

Paul's conversion was very powerful. The change in him was dynamic. Even his physical appearance began to change – he grew happier and stronger. He still worked on the farm and gardens. His conversion didn't make him any more practical, but what he now did he did with purpose and joy. I loved to go out to see him because I seemed to get so much joy myself from him. Paul was on the way to a new life – his mother's faith at last was rewarded. Her son, though dead, was now alive!

Some two weeks after Easter and Paul's experience, I had got once more weighed down by the burdens and problems of the work. I often found myself wondering at God's reason for calling such a weak person as myself. There were times when I felt so lonely and so misunderstood. I'm sure I made many mistakes and brought much of this on myself, but knowing that didn't make things any easier to bear. On this particular day everything seemed to go wrong. Someone who had promised financial support had withdrawn his offer, bills were piling up and everyone who came into my study had a criticism or a grumble. One of the staff members had just spent half-an-hour telling me about his problems with his wife and I was ready to throw in the towel. As this man talked to me, seeking comfort and advice, I longed for him to see *my* need and offer his help to *me*, but perhaps I was too sensitive or too proud, for I couldn't put my need across. Eventually he left me alone.

I cried out to God for help, I felt so weak, so useless. Then came a knock at the door. I summoned up my strength and called 'Come in!' – and it was Paul. He stood awkwardly half in and half out of the doorway. I sighed inwardly. 'Of all the people to catch me like this!' I thought as I struggled to climb out of the depression which was swiftly enveloping me.

'What do you want, old chap? I'm rather tied up at the moment!' I said as cheerily as I could. Paul came further into the room and stood in what can only be described as embarrassed silence.

'I don't want anything,' he whispered. 'I feel very foolish and don't know how to put this.'

My heart sank. 'Oh dear, what's coming?' I thought.

'You see,' Paul went on, 'I was working out there in the pig sties when all of a sudden I felt you were in need and God wanted me to come and pray for you.' He looked at me, a long loving honest look.

'Are you in need?' he asked, searching my face for an answer.

My first reaction was a proud one. I thought, 'I should be praying for you, young man, not you for me!' But the thought rushed away as I saw something in Paul's eyes which was so sincere. I said instead, 'If God's sent you to pray for me, then that's good enough – come on!'

I knelt down and closed my eyes as Paul placed his

hands on my head as he had seen me do so many times. For a moment there was silence, I supposed that Paul was searching for words. Then softly a wonderful peace began to flow over me, the tension melted away and I began to allow myself to receive from God through this young channel of his love.

Then very softly Paul started to pray. He prayed simply but powerfully and as he did so his hands shook my head gently. The problems were gone; I wasn't alone, God was meeting my need through his newest and most beloved messenger.

Paul stopped speaking and knelt down beside me and put a loving arm around me. I knew God cared.

As we stood up, with burdens gone, I saw this dear young man in a new light. He still needed my care and the ministry of Life for the World. He was still a baby and only a matter of weeks ago he had been an apparently incurable addict. Yet when he left my room that day I knew I could trust him with almost anything, certainly with myself, because Paul had stopped to care and to think and to love and to show it. He taught me that love could win and that even the most useless person was worthy of trust when they, like he, began to give. Paul was giving – and I was trusting.

In later years the yardstick God gave through Paul of when to trust a one-time addict always proved reliable. The one who begins to give instead of only taking has learned the truth, that it is more blessed to give than to receive, and trusting such a person becomes a joy.

My experience with Paul enabled me to know when to trust and how to share God's love with all who come for help.

In many rooms at Northwick Park we have pinned up a

Bible verse which has become a daily reality in the lives of weak and hopeless people.

'If any man be in Christ he is a new creature. Old things are passed away; behold, all things are become new.'

God has led many young lives to new strength and joy through the love which they found in our house of new beginnings.

Epilogue

We began writing this story at Northwick Park, the 'House of New Beginnings' itself. The wonderful thing is, that it is a story without end and this particular chapter was completed, not where it began, but in a new house. In 1976 we said good-bye to Northwick and made another new beginning at Cruchfield Manor near Windsor in Berkshire. It will need another book to tell that story of how, from those early days when God called us to reach out to young people in need, with absolutely nothing save that call, we have now actually been able to buy a lovely seventeenth-century house and dedicate it to the ongoing work of saving and healing young men in need of God's great love. How we were led from Northwick was as great a miracle as our finding it in the first place.

At the time of writing over four hundred young people have lived with us at Northwick and Cruchfield, the vast majority going out absolutely free men. Today those young men are scattered throughout the world, working in every kind of Christian and secular service: from carpenters to preachers, van drivers to university graduates and gardeners to missionaries. These young living testimonies to the power of the risen Christ are working in four continents and in almost every part of the British Isles. Already many more are coming to our new home and truly it can be said that 'the glory of the latter is greater than that of the former'! Addicts to drugs and alcohol can be set free; we are proving it day by day. Oh, yes, and in 1975 we opened a centre for girls, but that really must be another story.

Frank Wilson
Cruchfield Manor 1977

FOR THIS CROSS I'LL KILL YOU
Bruce Olson

'Don't go near them,' said the woman on the bus. 'They'll kill you.' But I was confident – and excited at beginning a new adventure.

Nineteen-year-old Bruce Olson knew God had called him to live with the Motilone Indians in the Colombian jungle. How did he survive the years of sickness, rejection and desperate loneliness which followed, until at least he won the confidence of the Motilone people, and learned how to bring them the message of Christ without destroying their culture?

It was for the cross that he loved the Motilones and became loved in return. But was it also for the cross that he or his first convert would die?

BREAKOUT
Fred Lemon with Gladys Knowlton

It was very quiet in my cell after the warder had escorted me back from the 'dungeons' – the punishment cells. I threw myself on the hard bed, a black bitterness of soul filling me. Tomorrow, I vowed, I would get hold of the sharpest knife in the mailbag room – and there would be murder done. Weary and tormented I pulled the coarse blanket round my shoulders and closed my eyes.

Something made me sit up suddenly. There were three men in the cell with me; they were dressed in ordinary civvy suits. The man on the right spoke.

'Fred,' he said, 'This is Jesus . . . '

Fred Lemon, a confirmed criminal, on the eve of attempting to break out of Dartmoor, unexpectedly broke out spiritually, and found this freedom far greater than that of the open moor.

This story of an East End child who grows into a violent criminal, simply and powerfully shows how criminality breeds and takes a man step by step into the abandonment of hell, and yet how Christ can meet a man even there.

Bestsellers by Juan Carlos Ortiz

DISCIPLE

Disciple tells of a spiritual revolution which transformed a Christian congregation in Buenos Aires, based on a new awareness of the total Lordship of Christ in the life of the believer. Sharing with the reader his discoveries about the meaning of discipleship, Juan Carlos Ortiz writes with shrewdness and humour. Gently questioning many of our most cherished traditions and habits of worship, he forces us to re-examine them in the light of revealed Scripture and exposes the shallowness of our claims to be followers of Jesus.

This is a challenging, at times controversial book. You may disagree with it, but you cannot ignore it.

CRY OF THE HUMAN HEART

Most Christians think they are living in the New Covenant. But they are not. Instead, they have made of the New Testament a set of rules and they are trying to fulfil these laws in the flesh. This misconception, Juan Carlos Ortiz believes, accounts for much of the spiritual defeat which Christians experience. They are frustrated, disappointed with themselves because they cannot fulfil that deepest cry of their hearts – to please God.

What is the way out of this dilemma? That is what this book is all about.

TOMORROW YOU DIE
Reona Peterson

Reona Peterson, of Youth With A Mission, heard God calling her to a mission of intrigue and danger. She and her friend Evey were to spread God's marvellous message of love ... even to Albania – one of the darkest atheistic countries in the world. This was a tense drama of calculated risk.

... A fascinating account of conditions inside the most atheistic country in Europe, by an eye-witness.

... Albania has been closed to the Christian gospel for more than 25 years and has been called the 'forgotten' communist country.

GIRL FRIDAY TO GLADYS AYLWARD
Vera Cowie

They made a film about Gladys Aylward's escape from mainland China with her orphan children. But what happened after the events of that film, 'The Inn of the Sixth Happiness'?

This book tells you. It is difficult to put down having all the ingredients of a bestseller – love, adventure, pathos and humour set against the exotic background of Taiwan.

Thousands have contributed to Gladys Aylward's work. Now the personal account of her later life and work can be read for the first time. The most personal account that has ever been published.

KATHRYN KUHLMAN
Helen K. Hosier

Thousands had new life and hope given to them by this remarkable Christian healer, and now the full details of her life are given in this book for the first time in the United Kingdom.

Her biography is a truly moving story of an elusive, enigmatic and extraordinary Christian with powers which stemmed from her implicit faith in the Father, Son and Holy Spirit.

This exciting narrative gives her background, her private life, her broken marriage, family, friends and where she came from and what she did.

YOUNG CHRISTIANS IN RUSSIA
Michael Bourdeaux and Katharine Murray

Michael Bourdeaux, through the facilities of the Centre for the Study of Religion and Communism, has gathered a wealth of information about young Christians in Russia today, and presents a surprising and heartening picture of a church which refuses to die.

CZECH-MATE
David Hathaway

Over the years the author took 150,000 Bibles and Testaments to Christians behind the Iron Curtain . . . One day he disappeared into a Communist prison.

This is his own account of his Bible carrying operations; of his arrest, trial and imprisonment; of life inside a communist prison; of the miracle of his release; and the part played by Harold Wilson and others in his return to freedom.

FORGIVE ME, NATASHA
Sergei Kourdakov

Teenage head of a Soviet police squad, Sergei Kourdakov led vicious attacks on Christian believers – until the courage of a girl he had beaten led him to defect to the West in search of the Christians' God.

Sergei died aged twenty-one. The book he left behind is a moving testimony to the power of God to change a life. It is also a unique and graphic account of childhood in a Soviet orphanage; and of a youth moulded by Communism, the system which shaped his ideals but which finally destroyed his illusions.

I FOUND GOD IN SOVIET RUSSIA
John Noble

One of the great testimonies of our time. 'An amazing account of the survival of Christian faith in the terrible conditions of the Communist prisons and camps' – *Billy Graham*

HEAVEN HERE I COME
Jean Darnall

'Heaven, here I come!' was Jean Darnall's exuberant response as a teenager to God's call. Wiser now, she still radiates energy and enthusiasm in a ministry which has taken her all over the world. In a refreshingly down-to-earth autobiography she tells how God has used her, and the many lessons he has taught her since her first cry 'Look out, Heaven, here I come!'

LIFE IN THE OVERLAP
Jean Darnall

Designed to help the reader understand the purpose of personal spiritual struggle. In presenting spiritual patterns of successful living for the Christian caught in the overlap between the Human Experience and Biblical Revelation, the author enables the reader to develop the desire to go and resolve these inner conflicts.

ELDRIDGE CLEAVER: ICE AND FIRE!
George Otis

Former Black Power militant, Eldridge Cleaver faces trial on charges arising from violent Black Panther confrontation with the police in 1968. Until last year Cleaver dodged trial by going into political exile. Finally, having visited the Meccas of his communist ideology, he settled in France, but it was not optimism that filled his soul but despair. In looking out at the vastness of the universe he came to believe in something more – God.